Mike and Carolyn LoGiudice

LinguiSystems, Inc.
3100 4th Avenue
East Moline, IL 61244-9700

1-800 PRO IDEA
1-800-776-4332

Skills: Grammar and Punctuation
Ages: 9 thru 14
Grades: 4 thru 9

FAX: 1-800-577-4555
E-mail: service@linguisystems.com
Web: www.linguisystems.com
TDD: 1-800-933-8331
        (for those with hearing impairments)

Copyright © 1998 LinguiSystems, Inc.

All of our products are copyrighted to protect the fine work of our authors. Copying this entire book for any reason is prohibited. You may, however, copy the worksheets as needed for your own use with students.

Any other reproduction or distribution of these worksheets is not allowed, including copying this book to use as another primary source or "master" copy.

Printed in the U.S.A.

ISBN 0-7606-0160-7

About the Authors

Michael LoGiudice, CPA, is an accountant who has the good fortune to be married to Carolyn. Mike used to punctuate his writing in a unique style that confused his readers. In fact, two of his high school English teachers went bald trying to improve Mike's writing. This book grew out of Carolyn's multitudinous attempts to upgrade Mike's punctuation skills so his readers could enjoy his scintillating content. The first step was researching and writing *100% Grammar* with Carolyn. *100% Punctuation* is their second publication with LinguiSystems.

Despite Mike's occasionally misplaced periods and colons, he is a forensic accountant ready to exhume financial records during lawsuits. He also scuba dives, gardens, reads voraciously, makes pottery, rides a Harley, and writes articles for a local paper.

Carolyn LoGiudice, M.S., CCC-SLP, is delighted to be married to Michael. It is well known that speech-language pathologists place a high value on communicating well. That's why she works for LinguiSystems, where she has edited and co-authored many materials for improving communication and problem solving, including *100% Grammar, The Listening Test, The Test of Problem Solving (TOPS),* and *The WORD Kits* for vocabulary and semantic skills. Besides correcting Mike's grammar and punctuation, Carolyn enjoys creative kitchen adventures, reading, traveling, and riding with Mike on his Harley.

Acknowledgments

We acknowledge and send heartfelt thanks to two very special people:

Paul Dallgas-Frey for his wonderful, zany illustrations

Margaret Hunt for her diligent proofing and technical guidance

Table of Contents

Introduction 5

Capitals
- Teacher Guide 7
- Quiz 12
- Overview 13
- Pronoun *I* 14
- Pronoun *I* and First Words in Sentences ... 15
- Names of People, Pets, and Characters 16
- Titles 17
- Titles of VIP's 18
- Relatives 19
- Brand Names 20
- Geographic Names 21
- Historic Periods and Special Events 22
- Books, Movies, Songs, and Shows 23
- Adjectives from Names 24
- Groups of People 25
- Dates and Addresses 26
- First Words in Quotations 27
- Interrupted Quotations 28
- Letter Openings and Closings 29
- Abbreviations of Names and Places 30
- Acronyms and Initializations 31
- Special Things 32
- Proofreading 33

End Marks
- Teacher Guide 34
- Quiz 36
- Overview 37
- Periods 38
- Question Marks 39
- Direct and Indirect Questions 40
- Exclamation Points 41
- Proofreading 42

Apostrophes
- Teacher Guide 43
- Quiz 46
- Overview 47
- Contractions 48
- Dialect 51
- Possessive Nouns 52
- Joint or Individual Ownership 55
- Organizations 56
- Words with Hyphens 57
- Indefinite Pronouns 58
- Possessive Pronouns 59
- Tricky Pronouns 60
- Certain Plurals 61
- Proofreading 62

Commas
- Teacher Guide 63
- Quiz 67
- Overview 68
- In a Series 69
- Nonessential Information 77
- Introductory Words and Phrases 78
- Interjections 79
- Prepositional Phrases 80
- Adverb Clauses 81
- Appositives 82
- Direct Address 84
- Parenthetical Comments 85
- Tag Questions 86
- Contrasting Elements 87
- Dates 88
- Addresses 89
- Letter Openings and Closings 90
- Titles 91

100% Punctuation

    Compound Sentences 92
    To Prevent Misreading 95
    Run-on Sentences 96
    Proofreading 97

Quotation Marks
    Teacher Guide 98
    Quiz 101
    Overview 102
    Direct Quotations 103
    End Marks 104
    Interrupted Quotations 105
    More Than One Sentence 106
    Indirect Questions 107
    Titles of Short Works 108
    Definitions in Sentences 109
    Slang or Special Words 110
    Quotation Within a Quotation 111
    Quotation as Part of a Sentence 112
    Proofreading 113

Colons
    Teacher Guide 114
    Quiz 116
    Overview 117
    Introducing Lists 118
    Long Quotations 120
    Restatements or Explanations 121
    Appositives 122
    Business Letter Openings 123
    Character Dialogue 124
    Groups of Numbers 125
    Titles and Subtitles 126
    Proofreading 127

Semicolons
    Teacher Guide 128
    Quiz 130
    Overview 131
    Separating Independent Clauses 132
    In a List or Series 134
    Proofreading 135

Hyphens
    Teacher Guide 136
    Quiz 138
    Overview 139
    Syllable Division 140
    Compound Numbers 141
    Prefixes and Suffixes 142
    Compound Adjectives 143
    Fractions 145
    Preventing Misreading 146
    Proofreading 147

Italics / Underlining
    Teacher Guide 148
    Quiz 150
    Overview 151
    Titles 152
    Foreign Words 155
    Words, Letters, or Numbers As Such 156
    Emphasis 157
    Proofreading 158

Answer Key 159

References 179

Introduction

Speaking English involves much more than putting words together in a logical order, based on English grammar rules. We also rely heavily on nonverbal language factors like volume, pitch, speaking rate, pauses, facial expressions, and even body posture to add meaning to what we say. For example, a wink or a long pause can change the whole meaning of a message.

When we are restricted to writing, we lose the benefit of all these nonverbal factors. The best tool we have to substitute for these factors is punctuation, a system of marks or signs that tell us where to pause and how long to pause as we read. Punctuation helps our readers know which words or thoughts go together and which are separate.

Good punctuation makes writing easier to read, but mastering punctuation is difficult for many of us. If the rules themselves aren't tricky enough, the usage variations among educated writers is enough to send the most ardent grammar fan scurrying to a preferred grammar reference now and then. For instance, all of these abbreviations for *miles per hour* are considered correct by various sources: *mph, MPH, m.p.h.,* and *Mph.*

Part of the confusion exists because punctuation rules change over time. Traditional rules pale as our eyes become accustomed to different usage, whether we agree with it or not. For example, many signs today read "Womens Room" instead of "Women's Room," exemplifying the decreasing use of the possessive apostrophe. Given current trends, how long do you think we'll officially distinguish *it's* from *its*?

Still, our students deserve to know as much as they can about using punctuation as a writing tool. Despite the variances in some punctuation usage, there are certain punctuation rules all competent writers are expected to know and use in English. The purpose of *100% Punctuation* is to explain these major punctuation rules to students. We hope the simple rule statements and examples, coupled with the lighthearted content of the activities, will grab students' attention and give them a shot at mastering basic punctuation in what they read and write.

Beyond completing the material in this book, your students will need your expert teaching. The Teacher Guides for each unit offer general principles as well as enrichment activities to supplement the activity worksheets. The tips for presenting each worksheet will shorten your preparation time and focus your lesson presentation. Here are some helpful strategies to apply throughout this program:

- Give the Quiz before beginning each unit so you know what your students have already mastered and what they need to learn. The Proofreading activity at the end of each unit also serves as a portfolio or outcome assessment measure.

- Supplement the activity sheets with the enrichment activities from the Teacher Guide in each unit. Add your own touches to these ideas, and encourage feedback from your students about which activities helped them learn and apply punctuation skills most effectively.

- The activity sheets in *100% Punctuation* include examples of the specific skill being taught. For each lesson, ask your students to think of additional examples before they begin the actual activity. Generating their own examples will boost their self-confidence and ensure that they grasp a particular skill before they need to apply it on the worksheet.

- When possible, present the activity sheets on an overhead as a group task, especially with more complex skills.

- Have your students exchange papers to proof their work.

- After your students complete an activity sheet, have them work in small groups to create a similar activity with original items. Then have groups exchange their creations for another group to complete. Finally, have each group proof its own worksheet.

- Designate a bulletin board to display some examples of the punctuation area your students are learning. For example, comic strips work well for both exclamations and commas.

- Ask your students to incorporate the current punctuation rule in their journal writing or other personal writing for the day.

- Write your own example of a particular punctuation rule at the top of a page. Then put this page on a clipboard and circulate it among your class. Ask each student to add an example and pass it on. Post the finished sheet where everyone can check it out. Are all the examples correct? Which ones are the most interesting? Why?

We hope your students experience *100% Punctuation* as helpful instruction, not as ironclad rules. As you share this material with your students, remind them often that English offers us great flexibility in what we say and how we say it, whether we speak it or write it. That's why there are several ways we can contrast ideas, clarify what we've already said, indicate pauses, and so forth. That's also why different writers use different styles for commas, abbreviations, and other punctuation marks. The key is to make the most effective use of the punctuation tools we have for specific writing purposes.

Teach your students to focus on an author's content and purpose more than an author's punctuation mechanics. As important as it is for students to understand punctuation rules, it's more important that they read well and find ways to express themselves in writing well. Skillful punctuation helps both readers and writers to share thoughts; poor punctuation gets in the way.

You are in a key position to teach your students how and why the skills in this book are relevant to them. You see their writing regularly, and you observe their oral reading. What specific observation can you share with each student that would improve that student's eagerness to understand and apply a point of punctuation?

We wish you every success in facilitating your students' smooth mastery of punctuation!

Mike and Carolyn

Capitals

Teacher Guide

Some rules for capitalization are easy to master, but some are tricky. It's easy to learn to capitalize the first word of a sentence, but difficult to decide whether or not to capitalize a person's title in some situations. As you work through this unit with your students, encourage them at least to recognize the writing contexts that might require capitalizing words. If they are aware of these contexts, they can easily check a good grammar text (this one, for instance!) or a dictionary for guidance.

Grammarians don't agree on all issues about capitalization. Where capitalization usage is inconsistent, use your discretion in presenting "rules" to your students. Some teachers present various opinions and leave it to students to select a preference in their own writing. Other teachers designate a preferred standard to minimize any confusion for their students. Also, some students are more comfortable with options and ambiguity than others who prefer to know and use "the rules."

If you or your school have a preferred grammar reference, share its guidelines and expectations with your students and encourage them to consult the appropriate books or resource information whenever they wish to know "the right way to do it."

Enrichment Activities

- Write a short message on the board, using all capital letters. Then rewrite the message, using lowercase letters except for the first letter of the first word. Ask your students to think about the difference in how these messages communicate. Which version is stronger? Chances are, your students will decide the all-capitals version packs more of a punch. Here are some sample messages for this activity:

    MEET ME AFTER CLASS TODAY.
    Meet me after class today.

    HAS ANYONE SEEN MY PEN?
    Has anyone seen my pen?

    WHO WANTS TO KNOW?
    Who wants to know?

    This activity points out the significance of using capital letters. A capital letter at the beginning of a word tells us that word is important, either because of the word itself (e.g., *England* or *Rita*) or because of the way the word is used (e.g., the first word in a sentence or a key word in a book title).

- Some people think a message in all capitals is like shouting or yelling. If that's logical, how would your students write a whispered message?

    Gather examples of creative usage of print to show various emotions or factors beyond the words or letters themselves.

- Write each word of a simple sentence on a separate index card. Capitalize the first word in the sentence and any others that require an initial capital. Mix the order of the cards and hand out one per student. Direct your students to arrange themselves as a sentence in front of the class. Then have them explain what clues told them the word order. Highlight the clue of a capitalized word to begin a sentence.

100% Punctuation

Activity Sheets

Overview, page 13

As you review this information with your students, encourage them to think of other examples for each type of word we capitalize. This page serves as a handy reference. Your students will be familiar with these capitalization rules by the end of the unit.

Pronoun *I*, page 14

Most of your students already know the pronoun *I* is always capitalized. This activity reminds them of that rule, and also gives them practice with noun-verb agreement.

For additional practice, have your students find quotations in news articles or other reading materials. Ask them to write each quotation on a separate sheet of paper, using the style of this activity sheet (replacing the word *I* with the speaker's name or identification). Have them exchange papers and rewrite the quotations using *I* appropriately and making any needed changes in the verb.

Pronoun *I* and First Words in Sentences, page 15

This activity gives additional practice in capitalizing *I* and reminds your students to capitalize the first word of every sentence. The riddle is about a wolf.

Names of People, Pets, and Characters, page 16

Read through the rules, examples and story with your students. Make sure they understand which words are included in each name in the story before they do their proofreading independently. Later, ask volunteers to share their made-up names for Joey's neighborhood. Be sure to share yours!

Titles, page 17

Caution your students that the first item is only started for them. There might be other words in the first sentence that also need to be capitalized.

Titles of VIP's, page 18

Grammar experts don't all agree about capitalizing people's titles. The traditional rule differentiates "very important people" from the rest of us, but status in today's world is more blurred than it used to be. Writers also need to consider the context of each situation; for example, the principal of a small elementary school would have more official status in that school's newsletter (capitalized title) than in a national news magazine (title not capitalized). This activity sheet uses only high-ranking titles that require capitalization in both traditional and modern usage.

Relatives, page 19

Many students have trouble knowing when to capitalize words like *mom* or *dad*. For extra practice, ask your students to write five original sentences requiring *Mom* or *Dad* and five requiring *mom* or *dad*.

Brand Names, page 20

Explain that the ® symbol after a brand name stands for "registered trademark." If your students use a word processor to do their writing, show them how to use this symbol to respect trademarks. Share your personal guidelines about using trademark symbols in written work for your class or your school.

100% Punctuation

Geographic Names, page 21

As a supplement to this activity, work with your students to list and describe all the local landmarks or parks in your area. You could also have teams each develop a small brochure designed to encourage tourists to visit your area.

Historic Periods and Special Events, page 22

The reason most historic eras and events are capitalized is that they are names of well-known events or times that retain a meaning across many years. For example, labels such as the *Iron Age* or the *Bronze Age* are based on technology characteristics. More recent designations, such as the *nuclear age* or the *space age*, have yet to pass the test of time that requires capitalizing the label.

Capitalizing quasi-historical or cultural references or events is often a matter of preference. Most people would capitalize the Kentucky Derby, but not everyone would capitalize the *cold war* or *pop art*. Share your own opinions with your students about capitalizing these types of words. Your students can also consult their textbooks, a dictionary, or an encyclopedia to help them decide whether or not to capitalize the names of specific events or happenings.

This activity also addresses the names of calendar items, such as months or days of the week. In general, the names of the four seasons are not capitalized. The exception is when seasons are personified, as in some poetry.

Books, Movies, Songs, and Shows, page 23

Capitalizing words in titles has almost become a lost art. Many people find it easier to capitalize every single word than to risk breaking the traditional grammar rules. Life won't end if your students overdo capitalizing words in titles, but they should at least be aware that there are traditional guidelines.

Many people forget to capitalize the small words *is, am* and *are* in titles. Another pesky area is phrasal verbs, such as *give up*. *Up* is part of the verb here, not a preposition. You wouldn't capitalize the preposition *up* in *My Hike up the Mountain*, but you would capitalize the word *up* as part of a phrasal verb in the title *Don't Give Up the Ship*. (No wonder many of us have trouble capitalizing words in titles!)

Adjectives from Names, page 24

Capitalizing adjectives derived from names, or proper nouns, is another grammar area that's often confusing. A dictionary is an excellent resource to resolve any doubts.

Sometimes an adjective derived from a name is capitalized to show a more specific meaning and lowercased for a looser, more generic meaning. For example, *Champagne* comes from the Champagne province in France; *champagne* is a similar beverage made somewhere else. Advise your students to consider both the dictionary information and the context of the word as they decide about capitalizing these kinds of words in their writing.

Groups of People, page 25

We capitalize the names of nationalities, tribes, races, religions, and languages to show respect. In current usage, some writers capitalize the racial terms *Blacks* and *Whites*, but others don't. A dictionary is the best resource whenever people are in doubt about capitalizing the name of a group of people.

We also capitalize the specific names of businesses, organizations, institutions, and government bodies. The trick here is to know which words to capitalize when you use a shortened version of an official name. The unique part of a name is generally capitalized; the broader or more generic part is usually written in lowercase, unless it's used as part of the official name.

> The **G**rand **H**otel opens next week.
>
> The **G**rand will have a restaurant.
>
> There are 63 rooms in the new **h**otel.

Dates and Addresses, page 26

Most of your students have probably mastered the rule about capitalizing the names of parts of dates and addresses. Some additional tips to point out here include using a comma to separate the parts of dates and addresses when you write them in sentences. This rule is highlighted in the Comma unit of this book.

Also caution your students not to capitalize the names of the four seasons: *fall, winter, spring,* and *summer.* These words are only capitalized as proper names, as in some poetry.

First Words in Quotations, page 27

This activity features capitalizing the first word that begins a new, direct quotation. Each quotation in this activity is complete and uninterrupted. The activity on page 28 introduces the rules for interrupted quotations.

Interrupted Quotations, page 28

Before your students tackle this activity, write the first example sentence on the board:

> "Did you know," she asked, "that Dana is my cousin?"

Ask students to rewrite this example on the board as many ways as possible, changing only the position of the words *she asked*. Some examples are included here:

> She asked, "Did you know that Dana is my cousin?"
>
> "Did you," she asked, "know that Dana is my cousin?"
>
> "Did you know that Dana," she asked, "is my cousin?"

Although some of these rewrites will sound more awkward than others, each one will reinforce the rule about not capitalizing the first word in the second part of a quotation that is interrupted in the middle of a sentence.

To simplify this activity sheet, instruct your students to think about the punctuation following each quotation interrupter. If it's a comma, then the quotation has been interrupted in the middle of a sentence. The

---

100% Punctuation Copyright © 1998 LinguiSystems, Inc.

first word in the second part of the quotation shouldn't be capitalized. If the interruption is followed by a period, the second part of the quotation begins a new sentence. The first word of that sentence should begin with a capital letter.

Letter Openings and Closings, page 29

To enrich this activity, label two columns on the board or an overhead: *openings* and *closings*. Work with your students to list as many letter openings and closings as you can. Highlight the difference in capitalizing these two parts of a letter. Words in a letter opening are treated like the title of a book, whereas only the first word in a letter closing is capitalized.

Abbreviations of Names and Places, page 30

Abbreviations save us time in both writing and speaking. In formal writing, though, writers should avoid abbreviations except for the following:

title abbreviations used with names
Dr. Ho, Ms. Kean

famous organization abbreviations
Y.M.C.A., NBA

Traditional grammar resources suggest capitalizing *A.M.*, often in small capitals:

Meet at 1:00 P.M. in the library.

Other resources suggest the following:

Meet at 1:00 p.m. in the library.

For this activity, tell your students to write the abbreviations as though they are for informal writing, since many of these items wouldn't be abbreviated in formal papers.

Acronyms and Initializations, page 31

Acronyms or initializations are words coined from the first letter of the important words in expressions or names, especially of governmental agencies. Most writers don't use periods with acronyms. Common acronyms include radio and TV stations, such as *KRON-TV*, as well as many technological terms, such as *AIDS (Acquired Immune Deficiency Syndrome)* or *LASER (Light Amplification by Stimulated Emission of Radiation)*.

Special Things, page 32

This activity sheet reminds students to capitalize the names of planes, ships, awards, statues, and school subjects that are languages or that include a number or letter in the course title.

For extra practice, ask your students to list their current school subjects, using appropriate capitalization. For more fun, allow them to generate lists of school subjects they wish they could add to the regular curriculum, including a brief description of course content.

Proofreading, page 33

This activity sheet offers your students a general review of many of the rules your students have learned about using capitals. Have them exchange papers to check their answers. If possible, display this activity sheet on an overhead so everyone can see it easily.

100% Punctuation

Capitals

Quiz

Cross out each lowercase letter that should be a capital letter. Write the correct capital above it. The first one is started for you.

1. ~~e~~(E)very time i eat strawberries, i get a rash.

2. "after lunch," dad said, "we'll see the brooklyn bridge and the statue of liberty."

3. when the civil war started, both the north and the south thought they could win.

4. our mayor wants everyone to agree not to smoke in the downtown area.

5. was abraham lincoln the first president of the united states?

6. my mom said she could drive me to my interview with mayor johnson.

7. is venus the farthest planet from the earth?

8. the title of the book i read is *darth strikes again*.

9. which dressing do you like better, italian or french?

10. i hope we have lunch at aunt julie's house again.

11. ms. cohen, principal of our school, will retire at the end of this year.

12. have you met uncle george before?

13. my sister loves mexican restaurants.

14. have you ever read *drums of the jungle* by tar zahn?

100% Punctuation

Capitals

Overview

A capital letter at the beginning of a word is a signal to readers. It tells readers the word is IMPORTANT. If the capitalized word begins a sentence, it signals the beginning of a new, complete thought.

Let's go for a bike ride. **W**e could take the long way to the beach.

A capital letter can also signal a person's name or the name of a specific place.

George **N**elson   **M**ount **W**ashington   **D**r. **S**mith

In this unit, you will learn about capitalizing these kinds of words:

- Names of people and characters — **K**im **C**hang, **D**onald **D**uck

- The pronoun *I* — Do you know why **I** like to sing?

- The first word of a sentence — **T**here's chewing gum in your hair.

- Titles — **G**overnor **D**ewgood, **D**r. **S**hotts

- Relatives — **U**ncle **A**l, **C**ousin **R**ita, **M**om, **G**randpa

- Brand names — **T**oys **Я** **U**s®, **D**oublemint®

- Geographic names — **E**ngland, **M**exico **C**ity, **P**alm **S**prings

- Events and documents — **C**ivil **W**ar, ***D**eclaration of **I**ndependence*

- Titles of books, movies, videos, songs, and shows — ***B**eauty and the **B**east*, ***F**orrest **G**ump*, ***T**he **L**ost **W**orld*, "**Y**ankee **D**oodle"

- Groups of people — **B**oy **S**couts, **A**frican-**A**mericans, **G**reeks

- Adjectives from proper names — **S**wiss chocolate, **F**rench fries

- Dates and addresses — **F**riday, **M**ay 15th   **A**lbany, **N**ew **Y**ork

- The first word of a quotation — **M**ike said, "**L**et's go for a ride."

- Letter openings and closings — **D**ear **U**ncle **P**ercy, **V**ery truly yours

- Abbreviations — **M**s. **S**ilvers, **M**t. **R**ushmore, **U.S.A.**, **B.C.**

100% Punctuation

Capitals

Pronoun *I*

A pronoun takes the place of a noun. The pronoun *I* takes the place of a person's name. Compare these quotations:

➡ Bert said, "Bert'll help you eat your pizza. Bert really likes pizza."

Bert said, "I'll help you eat your pizza. I really like pizza."

You capitalize the word *I* by itself or in a contraction because it takes the place of a person's name.

 Cross out each name that should be replaced by the word *I*. Write **I** above the name. Then see if the sentence makes sense. You might need to change the verb so it agrees with the pronoun *I*. You may also need to change other pronouns. The first one is done for you.

1. Patrick Henry said, "~~Patrick Henry~~ *I* ~~has~~ have just begun to fight."

2. Martin Luther King said, "Martin Luther King has a dream."

3. Bart promised, "Bart will not use his sleeve to blow his nose any more."

4. Rhett Butler said, "Frankly, my dear, Rhett Butler doesn't care."

5. Vanessa said, "Just ask for Vanessa, and Vanessa will be there to help you."

6. James said, "Anything you can do, James can do better."

7. Mary asked, "Does anyone mind if Mary leaves early today?"

8. As she played peek-a-boo with the baby, Jim's mom said, "Mrs. Garcia sees you!"

9. After winning the race, Tonio said, "Tonio is worn out, but Tonio is proud!"

10. Uncle Sam said, "Uncle Sam wants you."

100% Punctuation Copyright © 1998 LinguiSystems, Inc.

Capitals

Pronoun *I* and First Words in Sentences

Capitalize the pronoun *I* and the first word of every sentence.

 Rewrite each sentence of this riddle. Use capital letters wherever they are needed. Then guess the answer to the riddle.

1. i am an animal.
   _____

2. people say i'm a wild dog.
   _____

3. i am very smart and very loyal to the other animals in my pack.
   _____

4. my jaws are sharp and i run very fast on my toes.
   _____

5. i use my voice to howl or scare other animals away.
   _____

6. i can also use my ears, my hair, and my body to communicate.
   _____

7. my sense of smell is awesome!
   _____

8. if i meet a member of my pack that is more powerful than i am, i roll onto my back so we won't fight each other.
   _____
   _____

What am I? _____

100% Punctuation 15 Copyright © 1998 LinguiSystems, Inc.

Capitals

Names of People, Pets, and Characters

Capitalize the names and initials of specific people, pets, and characters.

➡ **D**avid   **M**ickey **M**ouse   **Mr**. **N**elson   **J**ohn **F**. **K**ennedy   **S**nowball

Don't capitalize common nouns that aren't really names, like *doctor* or *coach*, unless these nouns replace the names of specific people.

➡ My **d**octor's office is closed today.   *doesn't replace the doctor's name*
    Yes, **D**octor, I'll take all my medicine.   *replaces the doctor's name*

Don't capitalize a preposition or the words *a*, *an,* or *the* in a name.

➡ Kermit **t**he Frog   Attilla **t**he Hun   Alexander **t**he Great   Helen **of** Troy

✎ Proofread this story. Cross out each lowercase letter that should be a capital letter. Write the correct capital above it. The first one is done for you.

In ~~j~~**J**oey's neighborhood, everybody has a special name, like joey the fish. How did joey the fish get his name? The neighbors all agreed that joey ought to take showers more often. That's how joey the fish earned his name. Even joey's dog, spot, has a special name: spot full of slobber. teresa with the eyes is known for making eyes at all the boys. alex pass 'em all checkov is the driver's license bureau examiner. harry the slip connors can hide from anyone. manny the pickpocket is in jail for a while. tony fairway riso is always on the golf course. double dribble dale never could get the hang of playing basketball. What would your name be in joey's neighborhood?

100% Punctuation   Copyright © 1998 LinguiSystems, Inc.

Capitals

Titles

Capitalize a person's title if it comes before the person's name. If the title is abbreviated, start it with a capital letter and put a period after it.

➡ **Dr.** Judy Kelso   **Ms.** Finkle   **Mayor** Pitts   **President** Lincoln

Capitalize a person's title if it's used instead of the person's name.

➡ Thank you, **Mayor Pitts**.   Thank you, **Mayor**.

Don't capitalize a person's title if it's used alone or if it comes after the person's name.

➡ The **d**octor is sick today.   This is Ralph Pitts, **m**ayor of our town.

 Cross out each incorrect lowercase letter in these sentences. Write the correct capital letter above it. The first one is done for you.

1. ~~o~~fficer bronski gave a parking ticket to one of sister agnes's nuns in Big City.

2. The nun was parked in a no-parking zone when the officer gave her a ticket.

3. The nun asked the mayor, willy b. elected , to cancel the ticket.

4. mayor elected told the nun she must obey the law while she did good works.

5. The mayor wanted to make it easy for the nuns to park wherever they needed to park.

6. The officer said, "You could give the nuns special permits for their cars"

7. So mayor willy b. elected gave sister ann's nuns special parking permits.

8. The nuns could only use these permits in the special parking places.

9. officer bronski, the mayor, the nuns, and the prople of big city were pleased

10. mayor elected will probably be re-elected next year.

100% Punctuation

Capitals

Titles of VIP's

Titles of VIP's (very important persons) are capitalized whether they are used in front of names, alone, or after names. We capitalize these titles to show great respect. Many of these titles are for high-ranking officials in government. Titles of less well-known people are not capitalized.

➡ Bill Clinton, **P**resident of the U.S.A. from 1992-2000, came from Arkansas.
Carey Bartley, **p**resident of our school, wrote to our **m**ayor.

✎ Rewrite each sentence. Use capital letters where they belong.

1. Woodrow Wilson was the 28th president of the United States.

2. The president's leadership brought the U.S. out of isolation in 1917.

3. Under prime minister sir Robert Laird Borden, Canada had entered World War I three years earlier.

4. World War I started when Austrian archduke Francis Ferdinand was shot in 1914.

5. When Germany marched across Belgium to get to France, the British prime minister urged Great Britain to declare war on Germany.

6. In the U.S., president Wilson tried to keep his country out of the war.

7. Canada's close relationship with Great Britain made it more difficult for her prime minister.

100% Punctuation

Capitals

Relatives

Capitalize words that name relatives whenever these words are in front of people's names or when they replace people's names.

➡ My **A**unt Bea makes great grasshopper pie.
Grasshopper pie is one of the best things my **a**unt makes.

 Cross out each incorrect lowercase letter in these sentences. Write the correct letter above it.

Sally was spending the summer with her dad and aunt pam. Her aunt's house in the country was always fun to visit. Today was the day her dad had promised to take her fishing. Sally wasn't too keen on fishing, but she wanted to spend as much time as she could with her dad.

When her dad came downstairs, Sally was pleased that his tackle box was closed. At least the smelly, wriggly, slimy worms would be under cover. When they reached aunt pam's fishing hole, Sally was surprised that it was a pretty clearing along the bank of a stream. It would be a great place for a picnic, but a horrible place for hooking worms.

"It's time to bait the hooks," dad said. Sally forced herself to look interested as her dad opened the tackle box. Inside the box were pretty lures in all kinds of colors with beads and feathery things attached. Sally's father noticed her surprise and relief. Her dad explained, "No serious fisherman uses worms anymore." Fishing was going to be fun after all, as long as Sally didn't have to clean any fish!

Capitals

Brand Names

Brand names are the titles of products or things you can buy, like Kleenex® or Nike®. Capitalize each important word in brand names, but not common nouns that follow brand names.

➡ **Campbell's**® tomato soup   **Nike**® running shoes   **Diet Coke**® soda

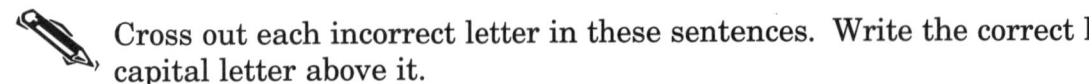 Cross out each incorrect letter in these sentences. Write the correct lowercase or capital letter above it.

Jim couldn't help it, he was a national-brand-name kind of guy. He used redken® on his hair, wore levi® jeans and ate mcdonalds'® fast food. Jim would wear any brand of shoes, as long as it was endorsed by a national basketball association player. He was the same way about beverages. He would drink gatorade®, but he wouldn't drink the milk from the local dairy, martha's farm. If coca-cola® bottled martha's farm's dairy milk, that would be different. If martha's farm had cool T-shirts or a fancy madison avenue ad campaign to market it, Jim might consider drinking their milk. What really makes Jim's mom mad is that Jim's grandmother, martha, owns martha's farm.

100% Punctuation   20   Copyright © 1998 LinguiSystems, Inc.

Capitals

Geographic Names

Capitalize the names of specific places or geographic features. Here is a list of major types of places to capitalize:

places or features	examples
continents, countries, states, provinces, counties, cities, towns, villages	**A**ustralia, **K**entucky, **O**ntario, **E**vansville
oceans, lakes, rivers, ponds, swamps	**P**acific, **L**ake **H**uron, **R**io **G**rande, the **E**verglades
beaches, islands, peninsulas	**C**oney **I**sland, **M**anhattan **B**each
mountains, valleys, deserts, forests, canyons	**M**ount **S**inai, **M**ojave **D**esert, **B**ryce **C**anyon
parks, dams, highways, streets, malls	**Y**osemite, **H**oover **D**am, **I**nterstate 80, **E**lm **S**treet
recognized parts of the world or a country	the **S**outh, the **N**orthwest, the **E**ast **C**oast

Capitalize direction words like *east* or *south* when they refer to a section of the world or a country. Don't capitalize these words when they refer to directions.

➡ Many countries import silk from the **E**ast. We headed east for 15 miles.

 Cross out each incorrect letter in these sentences. Write the correct lowercase or capital letter above it.

Last year, my family went on vacation out west. We saw the hoover dam, the grand canyon, the colorado river, and my sister's braces every time she smiled. Our first stop was mount rushmore in south dakota. It was kind of cool seeing the Presidents carved in stone. A bee stung my sister in custer state park. She screamed, and a herd of buffalo stampeded after her. Then we headed up into the rocky mountains. Pike's peak was so high, my sister got a nosebleed. In yellowstone national park, bears smashed my sister's camera. All in all, I'd say it was a great vacation!

100% Punctuation 21 Copyright © 1998 LinguiSystems, Inc.

Capitals

Historic Periods and Special Events

Capitalize special events, calendar items, and historic events or periods. Don't capitalize the names of the four seasons or names of recent or current periods.

➥ **T**hanksgiving **O**ctober **T**uesday **n**uclear **a**ge
   World **W**ar II **s**ummer **A**ge of **R**eason **B**ronze **A**ge

✎ Cross out each incorrect letter in this story. Write the correct lowercase or capital letter above it.

My Uncle Vinny isn't married, and my mom thinks that's a good thing. He never dates the same woman for very long. Last new year's day, he came over with a list of possible valentine's day presents for the woman he was seeing. Mom was not impressed. She told Uncle Vinny that anyone he was seeing in january would not be around in february. Uncle Vinny looked hurt. He said that sometimes he went out with the same woman for more than two months. Just last year, he took the same woman to the fourth of july fireworks that he had taken to the memorial day picnic in may. My mom pointed out that he was with a different woman by labor day in september. Uncle Vinny says he's just a modern man who should have been born in the age of romance. Mom thinks the stone age might be more fitting.

100% Punctuation

Capitals

Books, Movies, Songs, and Shows

Here are some tips about which words to capitalize in titles of books, movies, TV shows, videos, and plays:

- Capitalize the first and last words in a title.
    - *Morty the Worm*   *The Mystery of the Golden Mask*
- Capitalize all nouns, pronouns, verbs, adjectives, and adverbs.
    - *A Tale of Two Cities*   *Bert Is My Buddy*
- Unless they are the first or last words, don't capitalize these kinds of words:
    Articles (*a, an, the*)
    Coordinating conjunctions (*and, but, or, nor, for*)
    Prepositions with fewer than five letters (*over, of, on, at, for*)
    - *Once upon a Time*   *The Dragon of Lake Louise*
      Eggs over Easy   *Snails Are for Eating*

Rewrite each title. Use correct capitalization.

1. *a wrinkle in time* _____
2. *ralph the rascal* _____
3. *my name is bozo* _____
4. *taking it easy* _____
5. *a tale of two malls* _____
6. *grody gertrude* _____
7. *max is missing* _____
8. *mighty fine dreams* _____
9. *is anyone at home?* _____
10. *wind beneath my wings* _____

100% Punctuation

Capitals

Adjectives from Names

Some nouns and adjectives that came from proper names are capitalized and some aren't.

➥ **c**hina dishes   **v**enetian blinds   **G**erman shepherd   **G**reek salad

The best resource to help you find out if you should capitalize one of these words is the dictionary.

  Cross out each incorrect letter in these items and write the correct capital letter above it. Use a dictionary for help if you need it.

1. canadian bacon
2. plaster of paris
3. cheddar cheese
4. roman numeral
5. southern hospitality
6. swiss cheese
7. french fries
8. italian dressing
9. mexican restaurant
10. turkish bath
11. american habit
12. african violet
13. dutch oven

14. german measles
15. russian dressing
16. indian summer
17. japanese beetle
18. labrador retriever
19. arabian stallion
20. irish setter
21. mackinaw trout
22. manila paper
23. morocco leather
24. roquefort cheese
25. rosetta stone
26. gouda cheese

100% Punctuation   24   Copyright © 1998 LinguiSystems, Inc.

Capitals

Groups of People

Capitalize the names of races or ethnic groups, religions, and nationalities.

➡ **F**rench **A**merican **M**ethodist **G**reek **H**ispanic

Capitalize the names of businesses, agencies, organizations, cultures, and schools.

➡ **K**odak **R**ed **C**ross **Q**uaker **L**ongfellow **S**chool

Don't capitalize words like school, theater, temple, or church unless they're part of a specific name.

➡ Our school is hosting a dinner for **S**an **J**ose **S**chool.

✏ Cross out each incorrect letter in these sentences. Write the correct lowercase or capital letter above it.

Yesterday, we went to the International Food Fair at jackson high school. There was great food everywhere, and lots of it! Ben tried chinese pot stickers and vietnamese fish balls. Beth raved about amish dutch apple-crumb pie. Leon and Pat shared a greek gyro with a special sauce. Lavonne thought the mexican hot chocolate was the best she'd ever had. Matthew complained that all the food was gross, especially jamaican fried bananas. No one paid any attention to him, though, because he's such a picky eater.

I can't decide which food was my favorite. It sure wasn't the french snails with garlic! The hungarian goulash was pretty tasty, so I got the recipe for it. I guess the food I liked the best was japanese sushi. It was not only delicious, but also beautiful with many different colors and patterns. Actually, it was as much fun to watch the chefs make it as it was to eat it!

Capitals

Dates and Addresses

Capitalize the names of weekdays, months, streets, towns, cities, states, provinces, and countries.

➡ **Wednesday, April** 1   **Short Hills, New Jersey**

✎ Cross out each incorrect lowercase letter in this story. Write the correct capital letter above it.

I can't wait for friday, june 12, the beginning of summer vacation! I will be going to my dad's house in chicago, illinois. Most of the time I live with my mom in peoria, illinois. A lot of my friends are in peoria, but I have friends in chicago, also. We go to museums, shows, and the zoo when I visit my dad over the summer. It is great to see the chicago Art Institute, Adler Planetarium, and the Museum of Science and Industry. On the other hand, by the time I've spent two months with my dad, I miss my mom. When august 20 comes along, I'll be ready to head back to good old peoria, illinois.

Capitals

First Words in Quotations

Capitalize the first word in a direct quotation.

➥ Dad said, "**L**et's eat out tonight."

 Cross out each incorrect lowercase letter in these sentences. Write the correct capital letter above it.

1. Troy asked, "has anyone seen my comb?"

2. Angie whispered, "someone with red hair and freckles has a crush on you."

3. "class, please take out your math books," said Ms. Chang.

4. "there are pretzels on the counter for snacks today," announced Mr. Harvey.

5. Chad wondered, "why does Aunt Flo look like she has measles?"

6. The announcer shouted, "order your special alligator pencil today and save!"

7. "golly, we haven't solved any crimes yet today," sighed Batboy.

8. "don't worry, the Joker will be back soon," Bobbin said.

9. "is anyone interested in seeing my coin collection?" Horace asked.

10. "you've grown at least an inch!" squealed Aunt Rachel.

11. Leroy asked, "whose bright idea was it to climb this tree?"

12. Coach Nevins said, "take a ten-minute break, team."

13. "how does this can opener work?" Josie inquired.

14. "next time, check for a hole in your pocket before you put money in it," said Megan.

15. Jenny said, "never make a bet about how many worms you can eat."

100% Punctuation   27   Copyright © 1998 LinguiSystems, Inc.

Capitals

Interrupted Quotations

If a quotation sentence is interrupted with words like *he said*, don't capitalize the first word in the second part of the quotation. If the interruption is between two sentences, capitalize the first word in the second part of the quotation.

➥ "Did you know," she asked, "**t**hat Dana is going with Joel?"

"I'll tell you something," she said. "**D**ana is going with Joel."

 Cross out each incorrect letter in this story. Write the correct lowercase or capital letter above it.

"Just the facts, ma'am," said Sergeant Joe Monday. "tell me just the facts."

"well, when we saw the car coming," Mrs. Nonetoobright said, "We thought there would be trouble."

"What kind of trouble, Mrs. Nonetoobright?" asked Joe Monday. "what kind of trouble?"

"The kind of trouble," she continued, "That I don't want any part of."

"That's pretty vague, Mrs. Nonetoobright," said the sergeant. "can you be more specific?"

"The car was driving way too fast, and it was," she recalled, "Much bigger than most of the other cars in the neighborhood. I didn't want to know anything about it or who was in it."

"Why is that?" asked Monday.

"If I knew too much," she volunteered, "Then I'd have to get involved."

"What's wrong," asked Monday, "With being involved?"

"I knew if I got involved," continued Nonetoobright, "Some police people were bound to come around and ask a lot of questions."

100% Punctuation

Capitals

Letter Openings and Closings

Capitalize the important words in the opening of a letter.

➡ **Dear S**ir or **M**adam   **D**ear **G**randpa   **D**ear **M**s. **H**opkins

Capitalize the first word in the closing of a letter.

➡ **V**ery truly yours   **Y**our best friend   **S**incerely yours

 Cross out each incorrect letter in this letter. Write the correct lowercase or capital letter above it.

1.

555 Hanford Street
Anytown, FL 55514
October 14, 1999

The Hungry Pirate
2300 Seafood Lane
Port of Ocean, NJ 00020

dear hungry pirate:

I ate my last meal at your restaurant. I don't mean a meal I ate today. I mean it was the last meal I'll ever eat. Your peanut butter French fries were so gooey, they stuck to the roof of my mouth. They also stuck to my teeth. They also stuck to each other. I can't open my mouth!

I have been on intravenous feedings for a month now. A team of doctors and dentists is trying to figure out how to get my mouth open. We will send the doctor, dentist, and hospital bills to you.

very truly yours,

Notso Hungrynow
Notso Hungrynow

2.

dear aunt nita,

Thanks very much for the flannel pajamas for my birthday. You always know just what every kid wants most.

I hope you like what I'm sending you for your next birthday.

sincerely,
Karen
Karen

3.

dear paul,

Thanks for the gum. I found it right away this morning. Next time, please give me the gum before you chew it. By the way, you don't need to hide it on my chair the next time.

very truly yours,
SYDNEY
Sydney

4.

dear mom,

I'm sorry about the mess on the kitchen floor. I'm going to Theo's house after school. Hope you have a nice day!

your son,
Mike

100% Punctuation

Capitals

Abbreviations of Names and Places

Abbreviations are shortened words. Capitalize abbreviations of names or titles of people, states, places, companies, schools, and organizations.

➡   Los Angeles, California   **L.A., CA**

         Public School 42   **P.S. 42**

         LinguiSystems, Incorporated   LinguiSystems, **Inc.**

         Doctor Martin Luther King, Junior   **Dr.** Martin Luther King, **Jr.**

 Use the correct abbreviation from the box to rewrite each name or title. Some abbreviations may be used more than once. Use a dictionary if you need help. The first one is done for you.

Ms.	FL	NW	St.	N.Y.C.P.D.	P.O.
Gen.	N.	Assoc.	NY	ND	Ltd.

1. Collections, Limited   _Collections, Ltd._

2. Orlando, Florida

3. Post Office Box 42

4. General Grant

5. Mistress Louise Snodgrass

6. New York City Police Department

7. Saint Louis

8. Frick and Frack, Associates

9. North Tonawanda, New York

10. 354 Northwest Street

11. Bismarck, North Dakota

100% Punctuation

Capitals

Acronyms and Initializations

An acronym or initialization is a word made of the initials of the important words in a name or an expression. We pronounce some of these as though they are words (*ZIP* for *Zone Improvement Plan*), and we pronounce the letters of others (*V-I-P* for *VIP, Very Important Person*). Capitalize each letter of an acronym, and don't use any periods.

➥ Federal Bureau of Investigation **FBI**   sealed with a kiss **SWAK**

✎ Write the acronym for each item.

1. _____ all-points bulletin

2. _____ collect on delivery

3. _____ Thank goodness it's Friday!

4. _____ rest in peace

5. _____ acquired immune deficiency syndrome

6. _____ Mothers Against Drunk Driving

7. _____ video cassette recorder

8. _____ I owe you

9. _____ as soon as possible

10. _____ National Aeronautics and Space Administration

11. _____ estimated time of arrival

12. _____ prisoner of war

13. _____ répondez s'il vous plaît

14. _____ extra-sensory perception

15. _____ bring your own beverage

16. _____ most valuable player

100% Punctuation

Capitals

Special Things

Capitalize the names of planes, ships, awards, and statues.

➡ the *Titanic*   Academy Award   Olympic Gold Medal   Statue of Liberty

Capitalize the name of a school subject if it's a language or if it's followed by a number or a letter. Otherwise, don't capitalize school subjects.

➡ Spanish   Science 101   science   Algebra 2   history

Cross out each incorrect lowercase letter in these sentences. Write the correct capital letter above it.

Joan and Henry both go to hilton high school in brooklyn. They sit together in english literature b and in math. Last Friday, Joan and Henry went on a date. They took the ferry to staten island. The ferry wasn't as fancy as the *Queen Elizabeth*, but they had a lot of fun.

Henry said he'd call Joan, but two days have gone by and there hasn't been any phone call! Joan hopes Henry doesn't expect a gold medal for promptness. She figures that she'll go to the track meet on Wednesday. Henry will be running the two-mile relay. If he wants to be her Prince Charming, he'd better talk with her then. Otherwise, he'll be ancient history as far as Joan's concerned!

Capitals

Proofreading

 Now it's time to practice all the things you've learned about using capital letters. Proofread this story. Correct any errors in capitalization.

if a situation wasn't life threatening, it wasn't interesting enough for nick danger. "i like my situations hot," nick always said, "and my coca-cola® cold."

once, nick was in the jungle by the sao francisco river in brazil. he was traveling with native indian guides. the president of brazil was depending on nick to bring him important information. nick and his guides were traveling by boat through water thick with piranhas. Suddenly, the boat struck a boulder. nick's indian guides figured they were goners. not nick!

"grab the sides of the boat," nick shouted, "and hold them together!" nick was no superman, but he did command his guides' respect. they obeyed nick, now their fearless leader. they paddled to the shore before the boat broke up.

the president of brazil had given him up for lost when nick arrived at the meeting of the national congress. "sorry i'm late, folks," nick said, "but my boat sprang a leak on the way over."

100% Punctuation   33   Copyright © 1998 LinguiSystems, Inc.

End Marks

Teacher Guide

End marks punctuate, or signal, the ends of sentences. The rules for using end marks are fairly straightforward, and there are only a few tricks to mastering their usage. In this unit, your students will learn about using periods, question marks, and exclamation points correctly.

Enrichment Activities

- This activity highlights the flexibility of our language, both written and spoken, as well as the function of the three end marks. Write each word of a simple sentence on a separate index card. Then write a large period, question mark, and exclamation point, each on an individual card. Assign one card per student. Tell the students with cards they can earn one point for each way they can assemble themselves into a complete sentence or question, complete with an appropriate end mark. They may earn more than one point for the same sentence, as long as they can justify using each end mark.

  Your students will probably figure out quickly that they can earn extra points just by changing the inflection of the way they say a sentence. Here are some examples:

  It's my turn. (statement of fact)

  It's my turn! (pleased, surprised, or angry)

  It's my turn? (surprised or confused)

  Once your students are fairly comfortable with this activity, divide them into teams and let each team make up statements for the other teams to tackle.

- This activity is forced, but also fun and instructive. Rewrite a paragraph or two on the board or an overhead. Change some of the periods to exclamation points and some to question marks. Ask volunteers to read the passage, one sentence at a time, using the inflection suggested by each end mark. Some students may think of more than one way to inflect a sentence that has a particular end mark.

Activity Sheets

Overview, page 37

Talk about which example paragraph is easier to read aloud and why. Most people find it easier to read something that has appropriate punctuation, including appropriate end marks.

Periods, page 38

This activity gives your students practice with the most basic end mark, the period.

Question Marks, page 39

Your students need to differentiate using periods from using question marks on this activity sheet. All of the questions on this activity sheet are direct questions.

Direct and Indirect Questions, page 40

Some students may need extra practice orally with direct and indirect questions before they can tackle this activity sheet. Try tossing out indirect questions, asking students to change them into direct questions. Once they can do these revisions

100% Punctuation

easily, reverse the task. Ask a direct question, and challenge students to rephrase it as an indirect question. You could also write some common ways to begin indirect questions on the board for reference, such as these:

> I wonder . . . .
>
> She asked if . . . .
>
> Some people ask . . . .

Some students may need direct instruction in changing the order of the subject and verb when they revise a direct question into an indirect question. For these students, write each word of a question on a separate index card. Have other cards ready with the words needed to change the question into an indirect question, and have one card with a period and one with a question mark.

Assemble the question cards in the right order, with the question mark at the end. Next, add the cards to begin the indirect version of the question. Work with your students to arrange the rest of the cards in the right order, talking about which words change position so that the new sentence makes sense.

Exclamation Points, page 41

Exclamation points are seldom used in formal writing, yet often overused in casual writing. The frequency of exclamation points is more a matter of personal style and writer's intent than of strict punctuation rules. As long as your students understand the impact their use of exclamation points can have on readers, they're ready to take responsibility for the way they use this end mark.

Proofreading, page 42

Students' proofing corrections on this activity sheet may vary, yet still be correct, depending on their interpretation and their personal writing styles. The direct questions should, of course, end with question marks.

One appropriate version of the punctuation for this story is given in the Answer Key. Accept other logical appropriate versions.

End Marks

Quiz

Add the missing periods, question marks, and exclamation points to these sentences.

1. Uncle Ben, I wonder why some people never walk to get anywhere
2. Some people won't even walk two blocks
3. Do I sound like a grump
4. I don't mean to be a pain
5. It's such a waste of gas
6. Have you ever seen someone get in a car just to drive a block
7. Wouldn't it be quicker to walk
8. Do you notice how long it takes sometimes to find a parking space
9. Man, it's just not worth it
10. If I had a car, I wonder if I would use it
11. Would I change my opinion
12. Maybe I would
13. Hey, what a great idea
14. Uncle Ben, I wonder if you would loan me your car for a week
15. I'll take good care of it
16. Did you say you'll let me borrow your car
17. Thanks, that's awesome
18. I think I'll drive over to Randy's
19. After all, it'll be faster than walking three long blocks

End Marks

Overview

Punctuation marks at the end of sentences are like traffic signals. They tell you what's ahead and what to do. For example, if you see a period ahead, you know you're coming to the end of a sentence or a complete thought. An exclamation point and a question mark also signal the end of a thought.

Compare these two paragraphs. Which one is easier to read out loud? Why?

> My sister thinks she's the most important person on earth She hogs the bathroom for hours How can I use the bathroom I wish an alien would kidnap my sister

> My sister thinks she's the most important person on earth. She hogs the bathroom for hours. How can I ever use the bathroom? I wish an alien would kidnap my sister!

In this unit, you will learn about the three punctuation marks that signal the end of a complete thought:

Period •   It's the end of a sentence or a complete thought. STOP briefly, then go ahead if there's more to read.
> It's an hour until lunch. I'm already hungry.

Question Mark ?   It's the end of a direct question. STOP briefly, then go ahead if there's more to read.
> What time is it? Is it time for lunch?

Exclamation Point !   It's the end of an exciting thought. Put some excitement in what you're reading!
> Wow, it's finally time for lunch! I'm starved!

100% Punctuation

End Marks

Periods

Most sentences end with a period. That's because most sentences just tell information. There's usually not much excitement in a common sentence, so it gets the most common punctuation end mark, a period. Use a period at the end of these kinds of sentences:

a statement	We get our report cards today.
a mild command	Tell me about your report card.
an indirect question	I wonder what my report card will say.

Add periods where they belong in this story.

At home, I have to eat my vegetables before I can get dessert I don't see what the big deal is about vegetables My mom says that they are good for me If they are good for me, I wonder why they don't taste good *Good* should go with *good* If something tastes good, it should be good for you My mom says it just doesn't work that way Besides, she is the one who brings home the desserts Since she has the desserts, I have to do what she tells me

I wonder if we could get a dog that likes vegetables We could train it to sit by the table Then the dog could eat a carrot or some spinach if it fell on the floor Then we could eat more desserts

100% Punctuation   Copyright © 1998 LinguiSystems, Inc.

End Marks

Question Marks

A question mark signals you to stop briefly at the end of a direct question.

➡ Who are you? Why do you have gum on your nose? What planet are you from? "Why do I have to eat spinach?" asked Brad.

✎ Add question marks and periods where they belong.

1. What is the meaning of life

2. What is the answer to the ultimate question

3. Douglas Adams in the *Hitchhiker's Guide to the Galaxy* said the answer is 42

4. If the answer is 42, what was the ultimate question

5. I don't know why anyone wants to remember what six times seven is

6. Why don't things fall up

7. Which came first, the chicken or the egg

8. When you go to the store, be sure you get the right change

9. If no one is around to hear it, does a tree falling make a sound

10. When you can't see it, does it exist

11. If you can answer these questions, you're a philosopher

12. If you don't care, that's reasonably normal

100% Punctuation

End Marks

Direct and Indirect Questions

A direct question just asks a question. An indirect question tells about a question, but it doesn't ask a question directly.

> *direct* Where did you get that crazy hat?
>
> *indirect* I wonder where you got that crazy hat.

Add periods and question marks where they belong.

1. I wonder how long it will take to build that new building at the end of our street

2. How did they figure out how much lumber they'll need

3. I wonder how many new families will move in

4. Is the building going to have a store in it

5. Who would know how many workers will be building it

6. I'd like to know how they keep all the workers busy

7. When will it be finished

8. I wonder how we'll know when the first people move in

9. What if they have too much stuff to fit into their apartment

10. Dad asked if I'd like to be a building engineer

11. I wonder if I would like to build buildings

12. How will I know unless I try it for myself

End Marks

Exclamation Points

Exclamation points are like cheerleaders. They add extra pep or strong emotion to a sentence. An exclamation point can change almost any sentence or command into a stronger comment.

➥ *just plain period* A tornado can be dangerous.
   exclamation point A tornado is coming!

Too many exclamation points take away the punch of a message. Compare these passages:

> Pet tricks can be really great! My favorite one is Spike, the yodeling dog! When he hears Swiss music, he yodels like crazy! Spike is amazing!

> Pet tricks can be really great. My favorite one is Spike, the yodeling dog. When he hears Swiss music, he yodels like crazy. Spike is amazing!

✎ Add periods, question marks, and exclamation points where they belong.

I heard that our school will have uniforms next year   That's gross

Who says students all want to look alike   I don't understand how wearing

uniforms helps students get a better education   Lots of students already

get good grades   Wearing uniforms won't help kids study any better

What about the kids who drop out of school   Wearing uniforms won't

make kids want to stay in school longer   It might even make some kids

drop out earlier   Requiring uniforms is a crazy idea   We should

encourage students to help each other to learn, not to dress alike   If you

agree, please come to Room 102 to sign a student petition against uniforms

We need your help

100% Punctuation

Endmarks

Proofreading

Proofread this story to show what you know about endmarks. Correct any errors in endmarks in this story

Nedra couldn't think of the answer to the first test question! She wondered how she would pass this history test? She decided to skip the first question and go on to the next one. Oh, no, she couldn't think of the answer for the second question either. What was wrong! Why couldn't she think of any of the answers.

Nedra remembered how hard she had studied for this test. She had read the chapter three times! She had taken good notes. She practiced test questions with her stepmom and with her dad! Last night, she knew all the answers. Maybe what Nedra needed to do was take a deep breath and calm down?

Nedra closed her eyes! She took several deep breaths? Then she opened her eyes and read the first question again. It worked. She knew the answer right away. Nedra wondered why she had let herself get so uptight? After all, it was just one history test and she had studied for it. Nedra decided she would keep herself calm before she started the next test. Then the test would seem much easier right from the start?

100% Punctuation

Apostrophes

Teacher Guide

The word *apostrophe* comes from Latin and means "turned away" or "absent." It stands for missing letters in words. An apostrophe stands for missing letters in contractions, as in *he's* and *don't*. We also use an apostrophe to make a word possessive, as in *Ted's car*. Most English speakers today don't realize we use an apostrophe to show ownership because the apostrophe replaces the letter *e*. Years ago, English added *-es* to show ownership, as in *manes* for *man's*. Over time, the letter *e* was dropped and replaced by an apostrophe.

Currently, many signs and business logos omit the apostrophe from possessives, as in *womens room* or *teachers catalogs*. For the time being, most textbooks and grammar tests expect students to know and follow traditional apostrophe rules, and this book follows those traditional guidelines.

The variance in the use of the apostrophe, though, is an excellent example to share with your students to show that standard English grammar is alive and changing, however gradually.

Enrichment Activities

- Ask your students to gather examples of ads and other printed materials that use apostrophes. Talk about any deviations from traditional usage, and brainstorm why these deviations might occur. How important do your students think it is to use an apostrophe in contractions or in possessives? What difference does it make?

- Rewrite a passage that includes words with apostrophes. Leave out all the apostrophes. Work with your students to decide where to add any apostrophes, making sure a good reason is given for each use. Then compare your final version with the original. How are they the same and different?

Activity Sheets

Overview, page 47

As you review this information with your students, remind them to avoid using contractions in formal writing.

Contractions, pages 48-50

These activity sheets feature three types of contractions:

verb + *not*	don't
noun/pronoun + verb	Ted's, he'll
special words with missing letters	o'clock, 'cause

Explain that the word *apostrophe* means "turned away" or "absent" to teach the original use of this punctuation mark.

Dialect, page 51

Dialect often functions to establish the tone or setting of a piece of writing. Some people find dialect easy to read, yet others struggle with it. Some writers use dialect only for characters' dialogue, and others use it to add flavor to first-person narratives. Take this opportunity to make reading dialect easier for all of your students by showing them how to decode or translate it into their own speech systems.

100% Punctuation

For enrichment, write a sentence or two on the board. Ask a volunteer to read the passage, speaking in some kind of dialect. (Caution your students against mocking any particular group in their role-playing.) Allow the volunteer to change pronunciation and to substitute words, if necessary, to make the dialect as natural as possible. Then ask other volunteers to change the way the words were written on the board so that they reflect the actual way the volunteer spoke them. Here's an example:

> I'm almost ready to leave. I'll be back very soon.
>
> Ah'm fixin' to leave. Ah'll be back in jes' a minute.

Next, repeat the activity with a different volunteer, using a different kind of dialect.

Possessive Nouns, pages 52-54

Explain that earlier English used *-es* to show ownership. As our language evolved, people left out the letter *e* and substituted an apostrophe.

Grammar experts differ in their advice about showing possession for words ending in *s, x* or *z*. Perhaps the handiest rule is to follow the way each word is pronounced. If you add an extra syllable to show possession, add *-'s*. If you don't add a syllable when you mean possession, just add *-'* in your writing. Here are some examples:

> Hughes' (pronounced *huz*)
> Hughes's (pronounced *huz-ez*)
>
> Darius' (pronounced *dar-ee-us*)
> Darius's (pronounced *dar-ee-us-ez*)

On the first activity sheet, we have used the name Ross and chosen *Ross's* as the possessive form, although one could argue that *Ross'* is also correct. Share your opinions with your students about the options for this area of using apostrophes to show possession.

Joint or Individual Ownership, page 55

If this concept is hard for your students, try a more concrete explanation. This concrete demonstration shows the power the tiny apostrophe has in changing meaning. Call two students to the front of the room. Give each one a pencil, a book, or something more interesting. Ask a volunteer to write on the board who owns what, using this framework:

whose	**what**
(name)'s and (name)'s	pencil

What happens if you take one *-'s* away? Does the writing still show who owns what? Now take away one student's object, and tell the two students they must share the single object. Ask a volunteer to make the writing on the board match this change:

whose	**what**
(name) and (name)'s	pencil

Now reverse the order of the names, but put the *-'s* after the second name only. Does it still show the same thing?

Organizations, page 56

This activity sheet builds on the previous activity to show joint versus individual ownership.

Words with Hyphens, page 57

Hyphenated words follow the same rules as other nouns to show possession. Teach your students to focus on the last part of a

100% Punctuation

hyphenated word when they want to show possession.

Indefinite Pronouns, page 58

Your students will learn to add *-'s* to show possession with an indefinite pronoun. One tricky thing to point out to your students is where to put the *-'s* when the word *else* follows an indefinite pronoun. The *-'s* goes after *else*, not after the first indefinite pronoun, as in this example:

This is someone else's raincoat.

Possessive Pronouns, page 59

Possessive pronouns already show ownership, so there's no need to add *-'s* to them.

Tricky Pronouns, page 60

Many students have trouble discriminating *its* from *it's* and *whose* from *who's*. Refer back to the previous activity for students who need extra practice in identifying possessive pronouns.

If your students don't know which word to use in their writing, suggest that they write the sentence with a blank for the word in question. Then have them answer this question: Which kind of word is missing from the sentence—a verb, an adjective, or a possessive noun? If it's a verb or an adjective, use *it's* or *who's*. If it's a possessive noun, use *its* or *whose*.

verb or adjective	use a contraction with an apostrophe
	_____ raining. *verb*
	_____ juicy. *adjective*
noun	use a possessive pronoun; no apostrophe needed
	_____ slipper. *noun*

Certain Plurals, page 61

Traditional punctuation rules require that certain numbers, letters, words used as words, and signs use an *-'s* to show plural meaning. This activity sheet exposes your students to these traditional guidelines.

Proofreading, page 62

After your students complete their proofreading independently, review this activity as a class on an overhead. Ask volunteers to explain the need for each apostrophe.

Apostrophes

Quiz

Rewrite each sentence. Add apostrophes where they belong.

1. Everyones sure youre the teachers pet.

2. Thats why you got all As this year.

3. Its anyones guess why I dont get better grades.

4. Ive been bustin my bones this year.

5. Its hard to study at home cause its so noisy.

6. Dories and Sams friends are always coming over.

7. Id like it quiet by seven oclock every night.

8. Somethings bound to change my luck soon.

100% Punctuation   Copyright © 1998 LinguiSystems, Inc.

Apostrophes

Overview

Apostrophes are handy punctuation marks that show three things:

contractions   A letter or letters are missing.
                      I'm sorry, Ron didn't tell me you weren't coming with us.

possession   Someone owns something.
                      Grandma's chin

plurals   A number, symbol, letter, or abbreviation is plural.
                      Cindy got all C's this time.

In this unit, you will learn about using apostrophes with these kinds of words:

- **Contractions**

verbs	I didn't burp, Ms. Meyers. You're hearing things.
special words and dialect	We're fixin' to eat at six o'clock.

- **Possessives**

possessive nouns	Buster's dog won the prize.
nouns ending with *s* or *z*	All of the Jones's cats are weird.
joint ownership	Are you going to Kim and Nedra's party?
individual ownership	I like Tony's and Lou's posters.
words with hyphens and names of organizations	Chris loves his mother-in-law's visits. Mom works for Smith and Parker's law firm.
indefinite pronouns	My diary is nobody's business.

- **Certain plurals**

                                You get another turn if you roll double 4's.
                                You used too many um's in your speech today.

100% Punctuation

Apostrophes

Contractions

When we're just talking casually, we often shorten words. We might say "should've" for "should have" or "can't" for "cannot." In writing, we use an apostrophe to show how we've shortened words.

The most common shortened words are called **contractions**. A contraction is two words written as one word with a letter or letters missing. The apostrophe takes the place of the missing letter or letters.

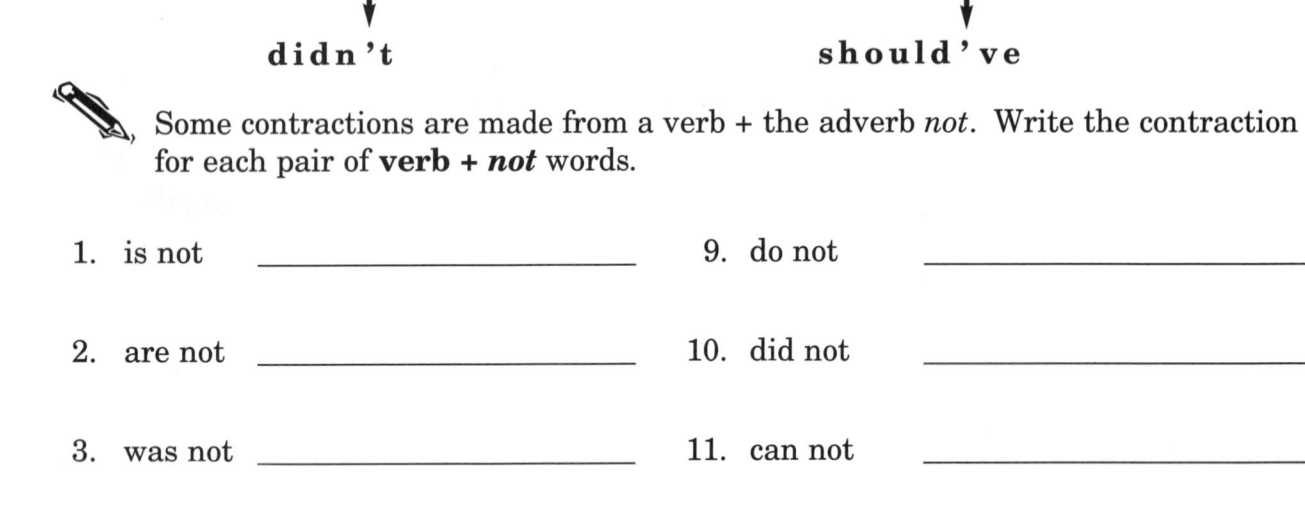

➡ did not   should have
   ↓   ↓
   didn't   should've

Some contractions are made from a verb + the adverb *not*. Write the contraction for each pair of **verb + *not*** words.

1. is not _____
2. are not _____
3. was not _____
4. were not _____
5. has not _____
6. have not _____
7. had not _____
8. does not _____

9. do not _____
10. did not _____
11. can not _____
12. could not _____
13. would not _____
14. should not _____
15. must not _____

One tricky verb + *not* contraction is *will* + *not*. Circle the correct contraction below.

willn't   **won't**

100% Punctuation

Apostrophes

Contractions

A contraction is a way to shorten two words into one word. An apostrophe marks the place where a letter or letters are missing from the contraction. Some contractions are made from a **pronoun** + a **verb**.

➡ she is ⟶ she's   they are ⟶ they're

✎ Write the correct contraction for the words below each blank.

1. _____ going to talk to Bill all night.

I am

2. _____ the coolest guy in our class.

He is

3. _____ the only one he ever calls.

I am

4. Dad says _____ only let me talk two minutes.

he will

5. Dad just doesn't realize _____ so important.

it is

6. I mean, Bill says _____ never call anyone else.

he will

7. Why can't Dad see how _____ improve my popularity?

it will

8. _____ just not fair.

It is

9. _____ never talked on the phone for more than ten minutes.

I have

10. Maybe _____ why Bill only calls me.

that is

100% Punctuation   49   Copyright © 1998 LinguiSystems, Inc.

Apostrophes

Contractions

Some special words use an apostrophe to stand for missing letters or numbers:

o'clock	of the clock	o'er	over
'sides	besides	'til	until
jack-o'-lantern	jack of the lantern	'cause	because
OK'd	okayed	'twas	it was

Fill in the contraction for the words below each blank.

_____ the biggest night of the county fair. If you _____
   It was   were not

there, it was _____ you had a darned good reason. The tractor
                    because

pull would start at 9 _____ sharp. It _____
                           of the clock   would not

end _____ there was only one tractor left. The motors on the
      until

tractors _____ be small. The motors _____
        would not   could not

be quiet. _____ be a lot of dust, noise, and danger. Everyone
          There would

_____ enjoy this event, but my friends and I _____
  would not   would not

miss the tractor pull for anything.

100% Punctuation

Apostrophes

Dialect

Sometimes writers use dialect to add flavor to their writing. These writers want the words on the page to suggest the way the words are pronounced in a certain dialect. If a dialect omits sounds in words, you can use an apostrophe to show which letters are dropped from the words.

> *standard English*   How is it going?
> *dialect*   How's it goin'?

This story is written in dialect. Some words are spelled to look the way they sound in the dialect. Other words use an apostrophe to take the place of missing letters. Underline each word that shows readers this story is written in dialect.

"I don't rightly know where you git that idee, ma'am," drawled Tex. "We bin tryin' to he'p these ol' boys as bes' we kin."

Maryanne smiled her sweetest Georgia smile and said, "Why, Tex, whatever could give you the idea that li'l ol' me would suspect a big, strong man like you? Y'all know that the guv'ner, bless 'im, wants me to investigate why this nasty ol' pipeline contract is so far behind schedule. Without that pipeline, the steel mill kain't open. An' the guv'ner did promise all them people jobs."

"Now, darlin', don't you worry yer pretty li'l head 'bout that pipeline bein' done on time," Tex answered. "We'll have that steel mill up and runnin' 'fore that 'lection."

Maryanne smiled sweetly, but her eyes sparkled like daggers. "Tex, deah," she warned, "you kain't hardly b'lieve how utterly unpleasant I kin be if y'all are even one day late!"

100% Punctuation

Apostrophes

Possessive Nouns

For most singular nouns, you just add **'s** to show ownership or possession.

➡ Drew has a rash.   Whose rash is it?   Drew**'s** rash

If the noun ends in an *s*, *x* or a *z*, you have choices about showing ownership. You may add either -**'s** or just -**'** at the end of the word.

➡ Tess**'s** picture or Tess**'** picture   the actress**'s** car or the actress**'** car

In each blank, write the possessive form of the noun below.

_____ mom was pleased that all the kids at school liked
    Ross

_____ new jacket. His _____ lining was red and
    Ross   jacket

yellow, the same as their _____ colors.
                             school

Another cool thing was the new computer _____ graphics.
                                            game

_____ Digital Dugout was the only place that had the game. At
    Leroy

the Dugout, the _____ reflection off _____ new jacket
                 light   Ross

matched some of the _____ graphics, as if the _____
                       game   jacket

designers copied the computer _____ design. But how could
                                 people

cloth match a computer _____ color and graphics? All the
                        screen

kids thought that the _____ designers must be awesome.
                     jacket

_____ _____ smile broadened as she whispered to
  Ross   mom

herself, "Yes, I'm awesome!"

100% Punctuation   52   Copyright © 1998 LinguiSystems, Inc.

Apostrophes

Possessive Nouns

You add an apostrophe at the end of most plural nouns to show who or what owns them.

➡ The babies have bottles.   the babies' bottles

Some plural nouns don't end in -s. To show possession for these nouns, add -'s.

➡ The people have a wish.   the people's wish

In each blank, write the possessive form of each plural noun below.

1. _____ bowling team
   women

2. _____ rights
   students

3. _____ group
   parents

4. _____ wings
   butterflies

5. _____ cheers
   fans

6. _____ orbits
   planets

7. _____ titles
   books

8. _____ retreat
   governors

9. _____ rules
   teachers

100% Punctuation

Apostrophes

Possessive Nouns

Most of the time, we use -' or -'s to show **who** owns something. Other times, we can use the same apostrophe rules to show **what** owns or has something.

➡ the worth of a dollar   a dollar**'s** worth

a delay of a month   a month**'s** delay

Rewrite each phrase to make it show possession. The first one is done for you.

1. the breath of a pig   _a pig's breath_
2. the pits of cherries
3. the warts of Jason
4. the quiet of a morning
5. a delay of a month
6. the strength of dental floss
7. the time of a year
8. the length of a hair
9. a journey of a day
10. a tentacle of an octopus
11. the passing of a century
12. the nostril of an ox
13. the worth of an idea
14. the width of a box
15. the price of freedom
16. the coming of spring

Apostrophes

Joint or Individual Ownership

When two or more nouns own the same thing, use -'s only after the last owner.

➡ Spot and Fido's doghouse   *Spot and Fido share the same doghouse.*

When two or more nouns each own their own things, use -'s after each owner.

➡ Spot's and Fido's collars   *Each dog has his own collar.*

This story is about the locker Mark and Sam share at school. Rewrite each sentence. Add the correct punctuation to show who owns each underlined noun.

1. Mark and Sam <u>locker</u> at school is the messiest.

2. Mark and Sam <u>jackets</u> barely fit inside.

3. The principal and vice-principal <u>inspection</u> of the lockers was today.

4. Maria and Angela <u>assignments</u> were neatly stored in their locker.

5. Maurice and Emil <u>backpacks</u> fit easily in their locker.

6. Mark and Sam <u>door</u> flew open when the principal lifted the latch.

7. About 444 baseball cards flew onto the principal and vice-principal <u>feet</u>.

8. The principal and vice-principal <u>eyeballs</u> were focused on Mark and Sam.

9. Mark and Sam <u>offer</u> was a Michael Jordan card to forget the whole incident.

Apostrophes

Organizations

Sometimes we talk about something that belongs to a business. If there is more than one name in the title of a business, use *-'s* only after the last name to show that the whole business owns something. If two or more organizations each own something, use *-'s* after each one.

➥ What's your favorite flavor of Ben & Tony's ice cream?

If each business or organization owns something separately, use *-'s* after each name.

➥ Ben & Tony's and Dairy Delight's chocolate ice creams are my top choices.

Rewrite each sentence. Add the correct punctuation to show who owns each underlined noun.

1. Barney and Bayleaf <u>Circus</u> is coming to town.

   _____

2. I wonder if they feed lions Roscoe Purity® <u>Cat Chow.</u>

   _____

3. Aunt Lucy works for Dewey, Cheatham, and Howe <u>law firm.</u>

   _____

4. She sued Setup and Fail temporary help <u>agency.</u>

   _____

5. Have you seen Hardly-Davidson newest <u>motorcycle</u>?

   _____

6. Mom took her car to Larson and Moore <u>repair shop.</u>

   _____

7. New York City and Chicago <u>crime rates</u> have dropped.

   _____

100% Punctuation   Copyright © 1998 LinguiSystems, Inc.

Apostrophes

Words with Hyphens

Some words have hyphens built into them, like *mother-in-law*. To make these kinds of words possessive, add *-'s* to the last part of the word.

➥ My sister-in-law**'s** birthday is tomorrow.

Rewrite each item. Add the correct punctuation to show who owns each underlined noun.

1. vice-president <u>sneeze</u>

2. great-grandfather <u>beard</u>

3. ex-mayor <u>socks</u>

4. sister-in-law <u>recipe</u>

5. president-elect <u>hobby</u>

6. brothers-in-law <u>jokes</u>

7. stand-in <u>performance</u>

8. AFL-CIO <u>rules</u>

9. vice-chancellors <u>portraits</u>

10. pick-me-up <u>power</u>

11. jack-in-the-box <u>handle</u>

12. June twenty-third <u>party</u>

100% Punctuation

Apostrophes

Indefinite Pronouns

Indefinite pronouns are words like these:

➡ another   anybody   anyone   either   everybody
  everyone   neither   nobody   no one   one
  other   somebody   someone   something someone else

To show possession with these pronouns, add -'s.

➡ Is this gum on my chair **someone's** idea of a joke?

✏ Rewrite each sentence. Add the correct punctuation to show who owns each underlined noun.

1. It was nobody <u>fault</u> that Jake won.

2. If it was anyone <u>turn</u> for something good, it was Jake's.

3. Jake was never somebody special <u>guy</u>.

4. He always had time to help with others <u>problems</u>.

5. Everybody else <u>time</u> was too valuable to help with his problems.

6. He got everyone <u>attention</u> when he won the lottery.

7. Now anybody <u>time</u> was his for the asking.

8. Jake wondered if he was living somebody else <u>life</u>.

100% Punctuation

Apostrophes

Possessive Pronouns

Possessive pronouns are words like *my, your,* and *our*. These words already show who owns something, so you don't need to add *-'s* to make them show ownership.

➥ This is Dan's book. It is **his** book.

✎ Proofread this story. Correct any errors in punctuation that show ownership.

We colonists came from a dying planet. Our's lush forests had long since been harvested for lumber. Oxygen, therefore, was a scarce resource. On our's home planet, huge utilities claimed a monopoly on all oxygen generation. They charged us outrageous fees for the right to breathe their's oxygen.

We crossed galaxies and solar systems to find our's new home. At last we landed our ship on the planet Vern. A dwarf sun's rays were casting their's warmth over the land. As space colonists, we believed our's right to control things extended beyond Vern's land. We wanted to guarantee all peoples right to breathe air without paying for it. Since there were so few people on Vern, their's need for breathable air was far less than their's supply. We planned to take their extra air for our's own use. The natives didn't seem to understand that we wanted to buy their's air. They didn't even know that anyone could own air.

100% Punctuation

Apostrophes

Tricky Pronouns

Lots of people confuse *it's* with *its* and *who's* with *whose*. What's the deal here? Once you understand exactly what these words mean, it's simple!

➡ **its** and **whose**   These possessive pronouns already tell you who or what owns something, so you don't need an apostrophe to show possession.

Whose pet is the silliest? My cat chases **its** shadow.

it's and **who's**   These contractions for *it is* and *who is* don't tell anything about possession. They tell who or what **is** or **is doing** something.

It's easy to see **who's** being silly now.

Write the correct possessive pronoun or contraction in each blank.

1. _____ doing what to whom?
   Whose   Who's

2. _____ the question Ms. Martin always asks the class.
   Its   It's

3. The question takes on a life of _____ own.
   its   it's

4. We are never sure _____ answer will satisfy her.
   whose   who's

5. When we get it right, _____ easy to tell.
   its   it's

6. She gives us a look like _____ all over.
   its   it's

7. She won't ask again, but we don't know _____ name she wrote down.
   whose   who's

8. That's why we don't know _____ answer worked.
   whose   who's

9. We all know _____ to blame.
   whose   who's

10. _____ just that we don't know if she knows.
    Its   It's

100% Punctuation

Apostrophes

Certain Plurals

Use -'s to show that special terms are plurals, including numbers, signs, letters, and words referred to as words.

➡ **V-8's** have more power than V-6 engines.

Oops, I confused the **+'s** for **-'s** on this math page.

Lex got three **A's** and two **B's** on his report card.

Your ***wow*'s** are getting on my nerves!

✎ Add apostrophes where they are needed in these sentences.

1. Officer Michaels and his dogs moved toward the suspected DC-10s on the runway.

2. These drug dogs were sensitive to the scent of PCPs.

3. The MPs formed a ring around the airplanes as soon as they landed.

4. All of the MPs had M-16s strapped to their shoulders.

5. The FBI had sent three GS-13s to brief Michaels, so he knew the case was big.

6. The files they provided had the 10-Ks for the companies who owned the airplanes.

7. On Michaels' routine SQ-25s, there was never this much firepower.

8. This was so big, he'd better dot all his *I*s and cross all his *T*s on this case.

9. These guys were armed to the 9s, and they meant business.

100% Punctuation

Apostrophes

Proofreading

Proofread this story. Correct any apostrophe errors.

Mike was a pilot for Ace Corporation. Ace Corporation owned his plane, and it was it's job to decide who would fly which routes. Mike thought he always got the worst assignments. He told a friend, "Everyone elses plane airlifts interestin people or grateful millionaires. Im gettin tired of always gettin stuck with the worst cargo to airlift. When its my flight, it's never a good assignment."

One day, Mike went to talk to the woman in charge of assigning flights. "Lets face it," complained Mike, "Im never in the runnin for the gravy routes! Theres gotta be a way to gimme some easy assignments!"

Thats how Mike was assigned to airlift some pets from Montserrats' disaster area. The Corporation figured hed have no one to listen to his's complaints. They also figured that a three-hour flight in a DC-3 with the engines roar and the animals noise would cure Mikes complaining.

Mike picked up a cat, a dog, and a parrot in Montserrat. The flight back was anyones worst nightmare. With a cats' meowing, a dogs barking, and a parrots cackling in his ears, Mike was anxious to land the flying zoo safely. Mikes landing was less than perfect, but it would do. It would also be his last for Ace Corporation, he decided.

100% Punctuation

Commas

Teacher Guide

The main purpose of commas is to indicate slight pauses in what we read. These pauses help us to identify chunks of information that belong together, whether we are reading to ourselves or reading aloud to someone else.

Enrichment Activities

- Rewrite a paragraph from a textbook or a story, omitting every comma. Display the passage on an overhead or the board. Ask your students to read it aloud in unison. Do they all pause after the same words? Are they more in unison for sentence endings than for places where commas would help?

  Ask your students what would make it easier to read in unison. If they don't suggest using commas to help with phrasing, point out this benefit of using commas.

- Rewrite a passage and add too many commas to it. Ask your students to read it in unison. What do they notice? What would they like to change? Why?

Activity Sheets

Overview, page 68

As you review this information with your students, talk about the ways commas give a visual signal that matches the natural pauses in spoken English. Have a student read each example sentence aloud, and ask the other students to notice how closely the reader's pauses match the commas in each sentence.

In a Series, pages 69-76

To introduce this series of activity sheets, ask your students to make a short list of things they'd like to add to the lunch menu or things they'd like to take on a trip to a space station. Write the list on the board. Then show your students how to write that list in a sentence, directing special attention to the commas to separate the list items.

Traditional grammar advises writers to use commas between all items in a list, no matter how many items there are. Other experts omit a comma between the last two items if the meaning is clear without it. The activity on page 74 explains this option. We recommend using commas between the last two items of a list if there are four or more items, and omitting a comma between the last two of three items if it's easy to understand without this comma. Share your own views about commas in lists with your students. Tell them what you expect from them in written work you assign.

The activity on page 75 deals with multiple adjectives modifying a noun. Two tests help writers decide whether to use a comma between the last two adjectives in front of a noun:

1. Rearrange the order of each modifier. If it makes sense in any order, use a comma between the last two modifiers.

   a cold, rainy day *(correct)*
   a rainy, cold day *(correct)*

   If it doesn't make sense when you change the order, don't separate the last two modifiers with a comma.

   a cold, November day *(incorrect)*
   a November, cold day *(awkward)*
   a cold November day *(correct)*

2. Insert the word *and* between each adjective. If the phrase still makes sense, separate the modifiers with a comma.

a cold, rainy day
a cold and rainy day } *same meaning*

a cold November day
a cold and November day } *not the same*

Nonessential Information, page 77

To introduce this activity, write the main part of the example sentence on the board:

Scamp hid under my bed until the storm stopped.

Explain that this sentence is complete. Then write the phrase "scared by the thunder" and ask your students where to insert it in the example sentence. This phrase adds information to the sentence, but since the information isn't critical to understand the main sentence, it is nonessential information. The commas set it off from the main sentence.

Introductory Words and Phrases, page 78

With your students, brainstorm all the words and phrases you can think of that start or introduce sentences. List each one on the board, followed by a comma, for practice.

Interjections, page 79

Alert your students that some writers use exclamation points more freely than others. The Answer Key lists probable answers, but allow students room for a difference in writing style in using exclamation points.

Prepositional Phrases, page 80

Review the meaning and use of *prepositional* and *parenthetical phrases* with your students before they complete this activity. Ask them to think of other examples of sentences that start with this type of phrase. Talk about which of these phrases should be separated from the rest of the sentence and tell why.

Adverb Clauses, page 81

Remind your students that adverbs tell how, when, where, or how much something happens. Adverb clauses are dependent clauses (clauses that couldn't be complete sentences by themselves) that often start with the words in the box on this activity sheet.

When an adverb clause introduces the main sentence, a comma separates it from the main sentence. No comma is necessary when the adverb clause follows the main sentence.

<u>When you leave</u>, shut the door.

Shut the door <u>when you leave</u>.

Appositives, pages 82-83

On the board, write the example sentences without the appositives and with the appositives to show that each sentence retains its overall meaning without the appositive. The commas set off less important or nonessential information. You could also show how appositives function by reversing the appositive and its referent in each example. What subtle differences in meaning are there when the appositives and referents are exchanged?

100% Punctuation

Direct Address, page 84

A direct address isn't essential information to a sentence, so it is set off by a comma or commas.

Parenthetical Comments, page 85

These nonessential parts of sentences are set off by a comma or commas. They are like asides in a play. Many writers also use a dash to separate parenthetical comments from the rest of a sentence:

You will — I hope — take a shower today.

The use of the dash is presented in the Fine Points unit later in this book. Use your own discretion in addressing the dash as part of the activity on page 85.

Tag Questions, page 86

Have your students practice turning statements into tag questions to show what tag questions are and how they are made.

Contrasting Elements, page 87

Write the example sentence on the board. Then erase the contrasting element to show that, like a parenthetical comment, a contrasting element isn't essential to a main sentence. A comma or commas set it apart.

Dates, page 88

Your students probably know about using commas in dates, but they may need to learn to add a comma after the year when they write a date in a sentence:

June 1, 2006, is the day I'll graduate.

Addresses, page 89

Just as the words *and* or *or* can replace a comma in a series, a preposition can replace a comma that separates parts of an address in a sentence.

Letter Openings and Closings, page 90

This activity uses an informal letter to feature using a comma after the opening. In formal letters, many writers use the traditional colon following the opening. A letter closing is always followed by a comma.

Titles, page 91

An abbreviated title following a name is like a parenthetical comment. It adds information to clarify the name, but that information isn't critical to understand the sentence.

Use this activity to review some common titles and their abbreviations. List each title on the board and ask volunteers to add the abbreviations. Then have your students think of a name, real or fictitious, to list with each title. Finally, ask your students to write one sentence using each name and abbreviated title, remembering to use commas to separate each name and title abbreviation and to separate each title abbreviation from the rest of each sentence.

Here are some abbreviations to include:

Junior	Jr.
Senior	Sr.
Doctor of Dental Surgery	D.D.S.
Doctor of Veterinary Medicine	D.V.M.
Registered Nurse	R.N.
Bachelor of Arts	B.A.
Bachelor of Science	B.S.
Master of Arts	M.A.

100% Punctuation

Master of Science	M.S.
Doctor of Law	J.D.
Doctor of Medicine	M.D.
Doctor of Laws	LL.D.
Justice of the Peace	J.P.

Compound Sentences, pages 92-94

Traditional grammar demands a comma before a coordinating conjunction that joins two independent clauses. In practice, many writers omit this comma if the clauses are short and if the meaning is clear without a comma. Note that this activity uses only coordinating conjunctions, not *because* or other subordinating conjunctions. That's because you don't often need a comma before a subordinating conjunction. Here's the difference:

> I'm tired, *for* I couldn't sleep. *(co-ordin.)*
>
> I'm tired *because* I couldn't sleep. *(subor.)*

The Answer Key in this book assumes your students are practicing traditional usage on the first and second activity sheets, pages 92 and 93, adding a comma before the coordinating conjunction.

The third activity, page 94, introduces the option of omitting the comma if the clauses are short and meaning is clear without it. If your students aren't sure whether to use a comma, encourage them to say the sentence out loud. If they pause before the coordinating conjunction, they should consider adding a comma for readers, even if the phrases are short. Compare these examples:

> I'll go but I'll be back.
>
> I'll go, but I'll be back.
>
> You call me or I'll call you.
>
> You call me, or I'll call you.

With the sentences above, readers need more context to be certain of the intent of each message, but the punctuation might signal slight differences in meaning. The point is for students to take an active role as writers, using punctuation as a tool to help convey the written message to readers as the message is intended.

To Prevent Misreading, page 95

Do this activity as a group on an overhead. Have your students read each sentence silently before any discussion to get an idea about what it means.

Run-on Sentences, page 96

In most cases, we lower our pitch more for a period at the end of a sentence than we do for a comma within a sentence. Teach your students to read their writing to themselves to help proof their punctuation as they write.

A run-on sentence substitutes a comma improperly for a period, a semicolon, or a conjunction. Some grammar resources refer to this error as a *comma fault*.

Since there are several correct ways to fix each sentence on this activity sheet, review the items as a group after your students have done their work individually. Sample answers are listed in the Answer Key, but accept other suitable responses as correct. This activity illustrates some of the flexibility of our language in writing the same message in different ways.

Proofreading, page 97

Your students' finished work on this activity sheet may differ due to the options for some rules about using commas. A sample of one acceptable version is listed in the Answer Key for your reference. Accept other correct responses as appropriate.

100% Punctuation

Commas

Quiz

Add commas wherever they are needed in these sentences.

1. On January 15 1963 Rev. Martin Luther King Jr. gave his most famous speech.

2. Dr. King led a march from Selma to Montgomery Alabama in 1965.

3. My oldest sister Gloria is more interested in historic events than I am.

4. Yesterday I told her "Everyone will laugh at you if you wear that dumb skirt."

5. She always says she doesn't care what people think but I don't believe her.

6. Well if that's what she wants to wear let her go ahead.

7. If Gloria had any sense though she would follow my advice.

8. Gloria who is fifteen thinks she knows everything in the world.

9. Gloria may be older than I but she has more to learn about things.

10. I know for example much more about shopping using makeup baking and boys.

11. All Gloria ever thinks about is history political events and dirty oily engines.

12. Uncle Jake from Las Vegas Nevada taught Gloria all about car engines.

13. He collects cars old motorcycles farm tractors and racing cars.

14. Instead of collecting old junk I wish Uncle Jake collected cool comics.

15. "Georgie I hope you've finished your homework" Mom said.

16. I told her I'd get back to it right away but it won't be easy.

17. How does my mom the daydream detector know when I'm daydreaming?

100% Punctuation 67 Copyright © 1998 LinguiSystems, Inc.

Commas

Overview

The comma is the most common punctuation mark. Commas are like fences. They keep things that belong together in a group and separate things that don't belong together.

In this unit, you will learn about using commas to do these things:

- Separate items in a series
    Dana's favorite sandwich has cheese, salami, mustard, and pickles in it.

- Separate two or more adjectives before a noun
    Please take your dirty, smelly feet off my chair.

- Separate two or more independent clauses
    We wanted to buy more popcorn, but the popcorn stand was closed.

- Set off words, phrases, or clauses that introduce a sentence
    So, like, have you seen Rick's latest outfit?
    As soon as you see it, you'll know why he has to stay after school again.

- Set off expressions that interrupt a sentence
    My sister, who is six, can already play the piano like a pro.
    You, my friend, are the winner of this excellent eraser.

- Separate parts of dates and addresses
    On January 14, 2007, my grandma from Dayton, Ohio, will be 100 years old.

- Signal the end of a letter opening or closing
    Dear Sue,   Very truly yours,

- Set off a title after a name
    Randy Wong, Ph.D., spoke to our class today.

You will also learn to be careful not to use too many commas when you write.

Commas

In a Series

A series in a sentence is a list of items. Use commas to keep each item in a series separate.

list style
➥ Jay's allergies
  milk
  oranges
  strawberries
  nuts

sentence style
Jay is allergic to milk, oranges, strawberries, and nuts.

Don't put a comma before the first item in a series or after the last item.

incorrect   Marta brought, yogurt, raisins, coconut, and cranberries, for a treat.

correct   Marta brought yogurt, raisins, coconut, and cranberries for a treat.

Add commas where they belong in these sentences.

1. You can choose red blue green or yellow M&M's®.

2. Call it candy chocolate treats or dessert, I like them all.

3. I'll eat pies cakes cookies and brownies.

4. *Large fat husky* and *ample* are words others use to describe me.

5. I prefer to think act and consider myself *impressive*.

6. I eat snack devour and inhale, therefore I am.

7. They want me on the wrestling football and tugging teams.

8. If it isn't eating sleeping resting or snacking, I'm not interested.

9. Coaches would just want me to jog exercise work and practice.

10. As someone famous said, "Give me cupcakes brownies and doughnuts, or give me death."

100% Punctuation   69   Copyright © 1998 LinguiSystems, Inc.

Commas

In a Series

An item in a series can be more than one word. Use commas only between whole items in a series.

➡ *incorrect* Zeke ate tossed, salad, French, fries, baked, beans, and celery, sticks.

correct Zeke ate tossed salad, French fries, baked beans, and celery sticks.

Add commas where they belong.

1. All right, I don't like wilted salad gooey okra stale corn bread or grits for lunch.

2. I'd rather have crisp salad raw carrots fresh corn bread and juicy watermelon.

3. If I can evaluate a lunch menu figure out what's wrong and propose a better menu, why not do it?

4. Too many people hold back say nothing and let problems grow larger.

5. If a menu includes poor choices unhealthy foods or stale choices, let's just say it.

6. If no one wants leftover mystery meat raw meat or smelly cheese, let's just say it.

7. I value simple honesty directness and absolute truth.

8. Yet I also know I should be open-minded kind to others and tolerant of others' preferences.

9. My brother says I am overly critical of others too judgmental and quick to find fault with just about anything.

10. He says I should spend more time praising others being grateful for what I have and looking for the good in everything.

11. I guess being positive about the cafeteria food complimenting the dietician and finding at least one thing to like on each menu would be a place to start.

Commas

In a Series

Words that are usually pairs of things that go together are considered one item in a series. Use commas to set off each pair of words that go together.

➥ *incorrect* Lunch today is spaghetti, with meatballs, tossed salad, garlic bread, with cheese, and brownies, with frozen yogurt for dessert.

correct Lunch today is spaghetti with meatballs, tossed salad, garlic bread with cheese, and brownies with frozen yogurt for dessert.

Add commas where they belong.

1. In tonight's game, you'll see the agony and ecstasy the effort the success and the drama of human competition.

2. For brunch, we serve rolls tea bagels and cream cheese doughnuts and coffee.

3. The music selections are country rock and roll blues or jazz.

4. You should pack your underwear shoes and socks shirts pants and a hat.

5. While returning from Cleveland, we encountered rain wind thunder and lightning hail and snow.

6. This is a land of milk and honey opportunity abundance and hope.

7. Diana cared for those without homes the rejected the sick and all others, too.

8. For lunch, I'm having a peanut butter and jelly sandwich juice and a cookie.

9. Deena's favorite makeup shades are light pink peaches and cream auburn and fawn beige.

100% Punctuation

Commas

In a Series

Items in a series can be words, phrases, or even clauses. Think of each whole item as one chunk of information. Use commas to keep each chunk separate.

➡ Standing in line, buying our tickets, and finding our seats took us an hour.

Our team was the first to beat Hoover High, the second to win three seasons in a row, and the first to have local TV coverage during our games.

✎ Add commas where they belong.

1. Wally planned to go to the store pick up the groceries and return home by noon.

2. That was before Ralph showed up took over his car and changed all the plans.

3. Ralph wanted to drive to the beach check out who was there and catch some rays.

4. When they got to the beach, a volleyball game was just getting started teams were being selected and they needed two more players.

5. Ralph loved spiking the ball digging for saves and blocking other players' spike attempts.

6. Wally enjoyed keeping score going for drinks and keeping out of the way of the volleyball.

7. Ralph thought they made a good team, since they stayed out of each other's way did different things and he got all the attention.

8. As he drove Ralph to the hospital, Wally agreed that Ralph's final shot would have been great made volleyball headlines and gotten Ralph a spot on the Olympic team if Ralph hadn't tripped over his feet.

100% Punctuation

Commas

In a Series

If all the items in a series are connected by the words **and** or **or**, you don't use a comma to separate them.

➡ We could watch TV**,** play cards**,** or tease my little brother.
We could watch TV **or** play cards **or** tease my little brother.

Jon keeps socks**,** old report cards**,** and his pet mouse in his top drawer.
Jon keeps socks **and** old report cards **and** his pet mouse in his top drawer.

Add commas where they belong.

1. At the hospital, Ralph went on and on and on.

2. He had to tell everyone about his great shot and his great moves and his spectacular ability.

3. Wally was glad to be out finished and on his way home.

4. Ralph could find someone else to take him home tomorrow and listen to his stories and sympathize with his incredible bad luck.

5. Wally liked Ralph when he wasn't bragging seeking attention or hogging the limelight.

6. When Ralph was unsure of himself or uncomfortable with the situation or with completely new people, he was hard to take.

7. He would overcompensate by talking loud or laughing boisterously or trying to be Mr. Charm.

8. If he would just be himself take it easy and let other people tell about themselves, more people would like him.

9. Wally didn't know if he should tell Ralph straight out or let him be or give him subtle hints.

10. Ralph was running low on friends and running out of chances and running out of time.

Commas

In a Series

You don't have to use a comma before the last item in a series if the meaning is clear without it. If you need a comma to make the meaning clear, add it. If you're not sure about the meaning, but you know it's the last item in the series, use a comma.

➡ *correct* The Birdman shakes, rattles and rolls.

correct The Birdman shakes, rattles, and rolls.

Add commas where they belong.

1. When you go scuba diving, be sure to bring tanks a wetsuit a mask a snorkel and a regulator.

2. Some of the different types of diving are wreck diving cave diving night diving and ice diving.

3. You can dive in rivers lakes quarries and the ocean.

4. Diving is for men women girls and boys.

5. There are specialty courses for navigation deep diving photography and rescue diving.

6. Some of the skills beginning divers learn are using a snorkel clearing your mask and doing the fin pivot.

7. There are ratings for open-water diver advanced diver rescue diver divemaster and instructor.

8. People dive in the Caribbean Pacific Atlantic and Indian Oceans.

100% Punctuation

Commas

In a Series

Use a comma to separate two or more adjectives that modify the same noun.

➥ *incorrect* Frankie the Ferret is an <u>adorable</u> <u>energetic</u> <u>lovable</u> pet.
  correct Frankie the Ferret is an <u>adorable,</u> <u>energetic,</u> <u>lovable</u> pet.

Sometimes the last adjective in a series is part of the noun. If you took the adjective away, the noun would change its meaning. Don't use a comma before an adjective that acts like it is part of the noun.

➥ *incorrect* Worms were everywhere that wet, rainy, spring <u>morning</u>.
  correct Worms were everywhere that wet, rainy <u>spring morning</u>.

Add commas where they belong.

1. Emil's incredible difficult long hike

2. a long hot humid summer evening

3. Gene's dirty old smelly slippers

4. an exciting free rock concert

5. a sudden loud piercing thunderclap

6. tangy fresh delicious brussels sprouts

7. a valuable engraved gold locket

8. an awesome mysterious surprising trick

9. the amazing new totally fat-free chocolate dessert

10. Marty's long boring campaign speech

100% Punctuation

Commas

In a Series

Sometimes a word in a series of adjectives modifies another modifier, not the noun at the end of the series. Don't use a comma to separate these modifiers that need to stay together to make sense.

➡ *incorrect*   Lisa has a cute, brand, new, fluffy, Persian kitten.

   correct   Lisa has a cute, brand new, fluffy, Persian kitten. (*Brand* modifies *new*.)

Add commas where they belong. The names of people are underlined.

1. There are many computer geeks powerful computers and network connections at the Micro Café.

2. Slide Rule Louie had cool moves fast fingers and the best brain on the block.

3. The delivery of keyboards color monitors modems and disk drives was received with excitement.

4. With new equipment, would Slide Rule Louie create new programs games software solutions or simulations?

5. When Louie starts cooking on the keyboard, you see flying fingers wild colors and cool animation.

6. As Louie walked into the Café, people stopped moved closer stared and tried to guess what he would do.

7. Among those around Louie were Brad CD Charlie Pat Mousepad Mike and Harry.

8. Louie had his books handwritten notes floppy disks and CD's.

9. The anticipation quiet and expectation hung heavily in the air.

10. Slide Rule Louie was ready to make awesome magic creative code and fun games.

Commas

Nonessential Information

Nonessential information in a sentence is words that add information, but aren't necessary to the meaning of the main sentence. Use commas to set off nonessential information.

➡ Scamp, scared by the thunder, hid under my bed until the storm stopped.

Notice the difference in meaning in the two sentences below.

➡ *essential*   The girl who is in ninth grade is the captain of our team.

There is more than one girl. "Who is in ninth grade" tells which girl is captain of the team.

nonessential   The girl, who is in ninth grade, is the captain of our team.

The main information is that the girl is the team captain.

Underline the nonessential information in each sentence. Then add commas where they belong.

1. My dog who is five years old is not the smartest animal in the world.

2. Last Saturday my mom's day off was a case in point.

3. It all started as you can imagine at breakfast.

4. Mom always planning wanted to know what we were going to do.

5. The *we* to be specific was the dog and yours truly.

6. Rather than keeping quiet as a smart dog would Bowser jumped up and wagged his tail.

7. Bowser's tail which is quite bushy started dusting the kitchen table.

8. In most cases especially when Mom's around that would have been fine.

9. Bowser's tail swept the dishes not yet cleaned that morning to the floor.

10. Then Bowser who has a huge tongue began licking the food off the broken dishes.

11. That my friends is just one reason Bowser hasn't won awards for intelligence.

100% Punctuation

Commas

Introductory Words and Phrases

An introductory element is a word or words that introduce, or begin, the main part of a sentence. Use a comma to separate an introductory element from the main sentence.

➡ <u>Well</u>, I'll see you later. <u>Come to think of it</u>, I'm late for school. <u>Yes</u>, I am.

<u>So</u>, what's new with you? <u>Why</u>, you look totally confused!

✏ Underline each introductory word or word group. Add commas where they belong.

At this rate we'll never get where we're going. You see every time my dad sees a garage sale sign, he has to stop. Why you never know when there might be an undiscovered treasure. In fact we have never yet found any treasures. However that doesn't stop Dad. No sir he checks out every single garage sale. Clearly there will not be a garage sale left unexamined by his eager eyes. As you may notice our car keeps getting loaded down with more and more things. Remember these things are not junk. No indeed they are potential treasures awaiting discovery.

Commas

Interjections

Interjections are words that express emotions, like *wow* or *yikes*. If an interjection is strong, use an exclamation mark after it. If an interjection is mild, use a comma after it to separate it from the next sentence.

➦ Yikes! What happened to my bike? Man, the wheels are all smashed up.

Use a comma to separate individual interjections that are joined into the same comment.

➦ Oh, yuck! I cracked the egg too hard.

Underline each interjection. Add commas, periods, question marks, exclamation points, and capital letters where they belong.

1. Watch out A space alien is landing

2. Oh my goodness it certainly has a lot of heads

3. Wow I've never seen such shiny boots

4. Fifteen feet that's a whole lot of shoes to buy

5. Wahoo It looks like a one-alien foot-stompin' parade

6. Wait If it has two stomachs will it have two belly buttons

7. Man how many eyes are in each head

8. Hmmm with four eyes how would it hook on eyeglasses

9. Hold on would you call it "eight eyes" if it had glasses

10. Watch it don't call the alien "eight eyes" if it can hear you

100% Punctuation

Commas

Prepositional Phrases

If a sentence begins with just one prepositional phrase, you don't need a comma after it unless the phrase is parenthetical (in my opinion, by the way, etc.) or you need a comma to avoid confusing readers.

➡ *parenthetical*   On the other hand, freckles are better than pimples.

no confusion   In the top drawer you'll find some safety pins.

avoids confusion   With chocolate, banana splits taste just right.

If a sentence begins with two or more prepositional phrases, use a comma after the last one in the series.

➡ Near the new store on the corner of Oak Avenue and Main Street, there's a place to post a sign if you lose your pet.

Add commas where they belong.

W. C. Fields (1880?-1946) was a great film comedian. Among the memorable things about his comedy style many of his sarcastic comments are still well known. On his tombstone his epitaph reads something like "All things considered I'd rather be here than in Philadelphia." With such an epitaph W. C. Fields didn't seem fond of Philadelphia. I on the other hand like Philadelphia quite a bit. For example near the historic district the mint is a fascinating place to visit. The cobblestone streets of the old town are now bumpy alleys and walkways. On my way home from school on some afternoons I take shortcuts through these alleys and walkways. Once I tried to ride through them on my bicycle. In no time as you can imagine I was bounced out of my skull. Maybe W. C. Fields liked riding on his bicycle. Above all other reasons that might be why he chose that epitaph.

100% Punctuation

Commas

Adverb Clauses

Adverb clauses often tell you about the setting of a sentence. They give information about where, when, why, or how something in the main sentence happened. Use a comma after an adverb clause at the beginning of a sentence.

➡ **While we watched the movie,** Stephanie made Gus a birthday cake.

The words in the box are adverbs that often begin an adverb clause.

when	before	so that	until	if	as long as
since	while	unless	whether	as	though
wherever	though	although	where	after	whenever

Add a comma after each adverb clause that begins a sentence.

Whenever we took my kid sister Harriet out in public she always embarrassed us. Even if you tried really hard you couldn't imagine more outrageous outfits than she wore. After a few embarrassing events with her my brother and I vowed never to go out in public with her again.

Since she knew we were concerned about her outfits one day Harriet dressed up like a fairy princess. Although that seemed harmless Harriet was no ordinary fairy princess. Whenever she heard a bell ring she would wave her fairy wand and bong people on the head. As long as we kept walking very fast no one got very upset. Until we stopped for the light on Fifth Street we thought we could get Harriet home without major problems. As if time had stopped this light would not turn from red to green. As we waited for the light to turn an ice cream truck came toward us. Before we could cross the street Harriet heard its bell. Though I'd like to continue this story my head pounds just thinking about it!

100% Punctuation

Commas

Appositives

An appositive is a word or words right after a noun that rename or explain that noun. Use commas to separate an appositive from the rest of the sentence.

➡ Your thyroid bone, or Adam's apple, protects your vocal cords.

Tonight we're going to a concert by Tubby Tomlin, the famous tuba player.

✎ Underline each appositive. Then add commas where they belong to separate the appositives from their main sentences.

1. Melissa was brought up by the right people the perfect manners people.

2. They the perfect manners people wouldn't even think of using the same fork for both salad and dessert.

3. When they eat or drink, they always hold the pinkie the smallest finger higher than the other fingers.

4. They say, "Good breeding the right stock always shows."

5. Melissa our sister always asks permission before leaving the dinner table.

6. She Melissa makes my brothers and me sick.

7. We the cool guys think manners that don't make any sense are stupid.

8. Melissa counters, "You my ignorant brothers need so much training that it's not worth the effort."

9. Wait a minute! Melissa our snooty sister has the same parents we do.

10. If having perfect manners is genetic inherited from your parents we're doomed!

100% Punctuation

Commas

Appositives

Most often, you could take an appositive out of a sentence without changing what the sentence means. Sometimes the appositive is so important to the meaning of the noun it modifies, you don't use a comma to separate it from the rest of the sentence.

➥ *no comma*   The book *Goosepimples* is on sale this week.

   comma   *Buzz*, our school newspaper, comes out every other week.

Notice the difference between these two sentences:

➥ *no comma*   My brother Chad turns 13 this month.
   I have more than one brother.

   comma   My brother, Chad, turns 13 this month.
   I only have one brother, Chad.

✎ Add commas where they belong.

1. Maureen wanted to see the movie *Action on the Bloody Frontier*.

2. John wanted to see a more romantic movie *The Promise of Love*.

3. Maureen wondered what John her friend was thinking.

4. Last week, Maureen had seen the movie *The Monster Who Ate Everyone* with Jason another friend.

5. Jason Maureen's preferred movie companion considered himself her only boyfriend.

6. Of all the boys she knew, though, Maureen's favorite was her friend John.

7. Perhaps she could transplant Jason's bloodthirsty movie taste into her favorite boyfriend John.

8. John the chosen boyfriend had no idea he was Maureen's favorite boyfriend.

9. John asked Maureen out to see the movie *Run, Girl, Run*, but she was busy.

10. After seeing Maureen with Jason, John a very confused fellow stopped asking Maureen out.

100% Punctuation   83   Copyright © 1998 LinguiSystems, Inc.

Commas

Direct Address

When you talk to someone directly in a sentence, you use the person's name or refer to the person directly. Use commas to set off direct addresses.

➡ Did you know, <u>Rachel</u>, that your left foot is bigger than your right?

Jason, my feet are none of your business.

✐ Add commas where they belong.

1. Karim we have to get serious about building this great pyramid.

2. We need more water Rafi for the workers.

3. The logs Faisal must be delivered over here.

4. Well, now, Joseph how many slaves will arrive today?

5. Yasir locate living quarters for the new arrivals.

6. Has the limestone quarry run out of stone Abdel?

7. Get enough slaves Ptolemy to ensure that there is plenty of stone.

8. I want you Habu to get the hemp woven into hauling ropes.

9. Amun of Thebes you bring me good news about the stone masons.

10. We will use your camels Sheik Hammad for hauling stone up inclines too steep for slaves.

11. Ah, Cleopatra it is no fun organizing the building of a pyramid.

100% Punctuation

Commas

Parenthetical Comments

A parenthetical comment is extra information in a sentence. Here are some expressions that are often parenthetical comments:

I think	I hope	I'm sure	for example	however
naturally	of course	in fact	by the way	after all

If you want readers to pay close attention to a parenthetical comment, don't set it off with commas. If you want readers to pause or give little emphasis to a parenthetical comment, use commas to set it off from the rest of the sentence.

➥ I hope you took your shower today.

You will, I hope, take a shower someday.

Sometime before picture day, I hope, you'll take a shower.

✎ Add commas where they belong.

1. Mary Jane in fact was the most sarcastic person in the world.

2. There was nothing and I mean nothing that she wouldn't say.

3. If it came into her head small head that it was she would say it.

4. It didn't matter who including family she offended.

5. She would smile such a sweet little smile naturally before she nailed you.

6. Then she met if bumping into someone is meeting Bad-Mouth Bob.

7. Bad-Mouth Bob as you may have guessed had the worst mouth around.

8. He wasn't just disgusting although he was that he was also mean.

9. He was to understate it downright cruel.

10. When they met, it was love although it seemed more like war at first slight.

11. Did you catch by the way the pun at the end of sentence ten?

100% Punctuation

Commas

Tag Questions

One way to find out if your listener agrees with you is to add a question at the end of your sentence. This kind of added-on question is called a **tag question**. It is tagged onto the end of a sentence. Use a comma to separate a tag question from the main sentence, and use a question mark at the end of the tag question.

plain sentence	*with tag question*
➥ You all want more homework.	You all want more homework**,** <u>don't you?</u>
That's a silly idea.	That's a silly idea**,** <u>isn't it?</u>
We don't need more homework.	We don't need more homework**,** <u>do we?</u>

Add a tag question to each sentence. Change the period to a comma and add a question mark at the end of your tag question. The first one is done for you.

1. We don't want me to get angry, <u>*do we?*</u>

2. You wouldn't want me to get wet in this rain. _____

3. I know you care for me. _____

4. It's true no one is happy when I'm miserable. _____

5. Let's see if we can find a solution. _____

6. I could ride in your nice, dry car. _____

7. That wouldn't get your seats too wet. _____

8. After all, I am your superior. _____

9. This is a fine situation. _____

10. You can't believe they drove off and left me. _____

100% Punctuation

Commas

Contrasting Elements

When you want to contrast things to explain what you mean, use a contrasting element. A *contrasting element* is a short phrase that starts with a word like *not*, *but*, *unlike*, or *never* and gives contrast to the main sentence. Use commas to set off a contrasting element from the rest of the sentence.

➥ Ted**,** unlike Brad**,** never burps in public.

Underline each contrasting element. Add commas where they belong.

1. The twins like fast-paced action games, not mind games.

2. They liked playing with people who couldn't tell them apart, not people who knew them.

3. These people thought the twins moved too fast for one person, more like two people.

4. Hide-and-seek, unlike dodgeball, was perfect for the twins.

5. Only one twin, never both, could be with the other players at a time.

6. When a twin was a hider, not a seeker, the plan would work.

7. The known twin would run away from, never toward, the hidden twin.

8. The seeker was being watched by two twins, not just one.

9. When the seeker got close to one twin, as opposed to the other, the fun began.

10. That was when the hidden twin could run, never walk, to home base.

100% Punctuation

Commas

Dates

Use a comma to separate parts of complete dates (month, day, and year) in sentences. You don't need a comma if it's just the month and the date or the month and the year.

➡ I was born on July 22, 1848, in San Francisco.

On Monday, May 12, 1997, a tornado touched down in our town.

Dad moved to a new apartment in April 1997.

We're having a party on September 20 at Mike's house.

✎ Add commas where they belong.

On March 10 1990 a statistics professor told me this math trick. If you ask 30 people for their birthdays, the odds are very good that two of them celebrate their birthdays on the same date each year. The first time I tried it March 11 1990 it worked like a charm. Something reminded me of this trick last week, just in time for our neighborhood block party. That would be a great time to try it again, even with only 28 people.

Once I explained the trick to everyone, we started making a list of our birthdays. I was born on August 26 1989 in Albany, New York. Geno Rizzo was born on May 10 1990 in Syracuse. His brother was born April 19 1992 and his mother was born April 21 1964. Kareem Jackson was born June 5 1989 in New York City. His dad was born January 6 1966 during a blizzard. Yolanda Royce was born on August 26 1990. It worked! Yolanda and I both share the birthday August 26.

Try it with your class or your neighborhood. Make a list of the month and date of everyone's birthday. I bet at least two people in your class have the same birthday!

Commas

Addresses

Use a comma to separate parts of addresses in sentences unless the parts are joined by a preposition.

➤ Margaret and Ray live at 1825 Oaks Street, Vero Beach, Florida, for ten years.

Margaret and Ray live at 1825 Oaks Street **in** Vero Beach, Florida, for ten years.

Add commas where they belong.

1. Is 235 North Main Street Springfield Missouri your current address?

2. You were clocked in front of 126 Maple Street in Wilton Iowa going 55 miles per hour.

3. From there to 360 Maple Street at the edge of town, Wilton is a 35-miles-per-hour zone.

4. I trailed you all the way to 777 Unlucky Boulevard here in Tipton Iowa.

5. You may pay your fine at 100 West Main Street Des Moines Iowa.

6. Your court date is September 12 1999 at 333 1st Street in Des Moines.

7. If you can't afford a lawyer, contact the public defender at 10 2nd Street Des Moines Iowa.

8. I suggest the safe driving school held at the Mercer Building 1515 26th Avenue Moscow Iowa.

9. The people at the Safety Institute on 300 Chevrolet Drive in Detroit Michigan want you to use your seat belts.

10. You may get your license after posting bond at 1223 Headquarters Avenue Wilton Iowa.

Commas

Letter Openings and Closings

Use a comma after the opening and closing of an informal letter.

➡ Dear Aunt Jenny,   Sincerely,   Your buddy,

✏ Add a comma after each opening and closing.

1. Dear Ms. Workmehard,

   The dog ate my homework. The attached gooey mass of almost paper is all that is left. Hope it doesn't make too much of a mess.

   Very truly yours,
   Sam Studious

2. Dear Dad,

   Send money. I can't tell you why. I don't think they'll be coming after you. You can trust me.

   Your loving son,
   Jerry

3. Dear Mom,

   Camp Swampfly isn't too bad. I think I'll enjoy it more once they let me out of the hospital.

   Sincerely,
   Anita

4. Dear Dynoblast,

   Please send me your latest catalog. Your chemistry sets are the best. This time I'll read the directions first. Maybe we won't need new windows again.

   Yours truly,
   Freddy Fearless

100% Punctuation

Commas

Titles

Use a comma after a name followed by a title abbreviation, such as *Rosey Hansen, R.N.* In a sentence, use commas to set off the title abbreviation from the rest of the sentence.

➥ Martin Luther King**, Jr.,** was named after the German religious leader Martin Luther.

David Marks**, Ph.D.,** wrote a book about how worms talk to fish.

Add commas where they belong.

1. Harry B. Finder M.D. had to identify a victim for the police.

2. Will B. Brief L.L.D. said the police wanted an answer as soon as possible.

3. Lou Zerman Ph.D. said his DNA testing could prove who the victim was.

4. Harry's wife, Ann E. Finder DVM didn't agree.

5. Ann thought Mary B. Quick Ph.D. could do the testing faster.

6. Harry and Ann called their friend Len D. Money CPA for advice.

7. Len D. Money CPA said both testers would charge high fees.

8. Mary B. Quick Ph.D. said Lou Zerman's work wasn't good quality.

9. Lou Zerman Ph.D. disagreed and showed a letter from Sylvia, a happy client.

10. Sylvia Lining MSW wrote that Lou had done a good job on her case.

Commas

Compound Sentences

An **independent clause** is a group of words that can stand alone as a sentence. Use a **coordinating conjunction** (*and, but, or, nor, for,* or *so*) to join two independent clauses together to make one sentence. Use a comma before the coordinating conjunction.

➡ *two clauses*   It's going to start raining soon. We'd better go inside.

sentence   It's going to start raining soon**,** **so** we'd better go inside.

Rewrite each pair of independent clauses into one sentence. Use a comma before a coordinating conjunction in each sentence you write.

1. There will be a test tomorrow. I should study tonight.

2. Mrs. Lincoln is not an easy teacher. Her tests are hard.

3. My favorite TV show is on tonight. I want to watch it.

4. I'm responsible for myself. I have to decide whether to watch TV or study.

5. Tonight's show is about dinosaurs. The test is on geography.

6. I like dinosaurs. I also like geography.

7. I could just watch the show. I could study before the TV show.

8. That is a good solution. There is no problem.

100% Punctuation

Commas

Compound Sentences

Use a comma before a coordinating conjunction that joins two independent clauses into one sentence (*and, but, or, nor, so, yet,* and *for*). Don't put a comma after the conjunction.

➡ *incorrect* Our dog chases birds **and,** we're glad she never catches any.

correct Our dog chases birds**,** **and** we're glad she never catches any.

Rewrite each sentence pair as one sentence. Use a comma before the coordinating conjunction you use to join the sentences together.

1. We had been gone for days. Our dog, Rascal, was happy to see us.

2. We opened the car door. Rascal jumped right in.

3. The window wasn't open very far. Rascal couldn't jump out.

4. He slobbered everywhere. I'd have to clean up the drool all over the car.

5. His hair was all over the back seat. Someone would have to vacuum it.

6. I offered to clean up the drool. My brother didn't offer to do anything.

7. Rascal started barking. Mom told him to calm down.

8. We laughed. Mom didn't see the humor.

100% Punctuation

Commas

Compound Sentences

Usually, you use a comma and a coordinating conjunction to join two independent clauses into one sentence. If both clauses are short, you can omit the comma if the meaning is clear without it. The coordinating conjunctions *and* and *or* are often used for this type of compound sentence.

> *no comma needed* You lead **and** I'll follow.
>
> *comma needed* You are the perfect choice to lead**, and** I will gladly follow.
>
> *no comma needed* Don't shout **or** I'll hold my breath.
>
> *comma needed* Don't even dare to shout**, or** I'll hold my breath forever.

Rewrite each sentence pair as one sentence. Use a coordinating conjunction to join the sentences, and add commas where you need them.

1. I'm not a picky eater. I'll try anything.

2. You took that smelly cheese out. I'm leaving.

3. I said I'd eat anything. I was wrong.

4. I won't eat that smelly cheese. It smells as bad as it looks.

5. Put that ugly, smelly cheese away. I'll leave.

6. Now the whole room stinks. I can't stay.

7. You're going to open a window. You think the smell will go away quickly.

8. You ate some of the stinky cheese. Your breath still smells awful.

100% Punctuation

Commas

To Prevent Misreading

Use a comma to separate words that might be confusing without the comma.

➥ *confusing*   Before the party seemed like a good idea.

   correct   Before, the party seemed like a good idea.

Add commas where they are needed.

1. Once the mixture is blended add the sifted flour.

2. Aware of the noise the band leader closed the door.

3. She who laughs last laughs best.

4. But for a tense second the audience enjoyed the performance.

5. A ring on the other hand would be too expensive.

6. Once discovered caves with fine caverns can become famous.

7. Now refreshed the hikers continued their dangerous climb.

8. Earlier bus passengers could get change when they paid their fares.

9. Once revolutionary telephones and TV's have become routine home equipment.

10. While we were kicking the principal visited our swimming training.

11. With children around sharp things can be dangerous.

12. For once Brad's shoes are tied and his socks are clean.

13. Not knowing for sure I guessed at the answer.

14. By the way she already asked someone to walk her home.

15. Suddenly famous Rachel had to wear sunglasses and a hat to avoid her fans.

16. With exercise athletes' muscles get even stronger.

100% Punctuation

Commas

Run-on Sentences

A **run-on sentence** is two or more sentences joined incorrectly into one sentence. Other names for a run-on sentence are a **run-together sentence** and a **fused sentence**. To fix this kind of error, break the run-on sentence into two or more sentences or use a conjunction to join the sentences correctly.

➡ *run-on* Deb has sung in school concerts, she has never sung on TV before.
corrected Deb has sung in school concerts. She has never sung on TV before.
corrected Deb has sung in school concerts, **but** she has never sung on TV before.
corrected **Although** Deb has sung in school concerts, she has never sung on TV before.

On a separate piece of paper, rewrite each run-on sentence correctly. Use commas where they belong.

1. I am always late for the class after gym class, the room is clear on the other side of the school.

2. If I don't take a shower, I can make it to class, everyone in the class would wish I didn't make it.

3. My choices are to be late or to be stinky, that is not much of a choice.

4. In the summer, I can go outside and take a shortcut, that doesn't help me in the winter.

5. I think the principal set up my schedule, I always get in trouble, it seems I have to visit her every day.

6. She said she doesn't want to see me in her office again for being late, I asked her how I can get from one end of the school to the other.

7. The principal looked at my schedule, she asked how it got set up this way.

8. She moved my gym class to the end of the day, that solved the problem.

9. Maybe the principal didn't set up my schedule to get me in trouble, she was good about fixing it.

10. I guess principals can be helpful, too, none of my classmates had better hear me say that, I'll lose friends forever.

Commas

Proofreading

Proofread this story. Add commas where they belong.

I'll never forget Saturday, June 11, 1994. It all started out normally enough, and I thought it would be a lazy summer Saturday. That was before Larry Minton, Ph.D., showed up at my apartment at 522 West 23rd Street, Minot, South Dakota. You wouldn't think that one person could spoil a day, would you? Well, you just don't know Dr. Minton. Someday, maybe even in this century, I'll be able to meet with Minton without any disasters. If you think we were going to have a normal meeting that Saturday, you're wrong.

It didn't matter to Larry that I had to mow the lawn, clean the garage, pick up the mail, and get groceries. No, that conceited, arrogant, pushy, vain Larry wanted his special problem to take center stage. Although I tried to tell him I was too busy for another one of his adventures, he told me we were off to the Amazon rain forest in Brazil. He had my ticket, and all I had to do was pack a few things for jungle hiking.

"You know," I protested, "I have a life too!" Larry explained that he had contacted all of my teachers, and they agreed that a trip to the Amazon rain forest would be an educational experience. They would, furthermore, be happy to allow me to accompany such a renowned anthropologist as Dr. Lawrence Minton.

Well, there you have it, one minute I was going to the grocery store, and the next minute I was on my way to Brazil. The funny thing is, that was the most planned, normal, sane thing that happened to us on that adventure.

100% Punctuation   97   Copyright © 1998 LinguiSystems, Inc.

Quotation Marks

Teacher Guide

The primary use of quotation marks is to set off a speaker's actual words. Other uses your students will learn to use in this unit include the following:

- titles of short works or parts of works
- definitions within sentences
- marking slang or unusual terms

Enrichment Activities

- Bring in some comic strips. Remind your students that quotation marks signal the exact words of speakers. Write the dialogue for one strip on the board or an overhead, writing only one dialogue bubble per line. Then have your students act the comic strip. Afterwards, work with your students to rewrite the dialogue as though it were part of a passage without pictures. Add phrases such as "Dennis replied" or "said Garfield."

  Once the group is satisfied with the content and style of the passage, add the quotation marks and any other necessary punctuation. Ask your students to describe the function of quotation marks: to make it obvious which words in text are spoken by characters.

  Then divide your class into small groups. Give each group one comic strip to rewrite as text without pictures, adding words and punctuation as necessary. As the groups work, circulate to lend a hand with specific punctuation. Since some of the fine points of using quotation marks may be unfamiliar to your students at this point, use this activity as an introduction to the basic usefulness of quotation marks rather than a lesson in any specifics.

- Assign small groups of students simple conversational situations to role-play. Phone interactions work well here. Ask each group to write the script and enact the scene for the class. Once each group has performed, have the groups exchange scripts and rewrite the script as text. Point out that, in text, each new speaker's quotation starts a new paragraph.

As your students write, encourage them to add interesting information to the introductory phrases or source words for each quotation, rather than just writing "he said" or "she asked." Here are some examples that add hints about the speakers' emotions or actions:

> Max blushed and looked at his feet as he mumbled, ". . . ."

> With eyes as round as saucers, Tina yelled, ". . . ."

> ". . . ," gasped Oglah, clutching his claw tightly.

Activity Sheets

Overview, page 102

The information points out that quotation marks come in pairs, one for opening and one for closing each quotation. In writing and in some type styles, the opening quotation marks are like two upside-down commas and the closing marks are like two raised commas. Other type styles use one symbol for both sets, usually in a sans-serif type font such as Helvetica.

Direct Quotations, page 103

This book uses the term *source words* to refer to the words introducing a quotation or identifying the speaker of those words. Be sure your students understand what source words are and how they function in text.

End Marks, page 104

Since the use of exclamation points is largely a matter of personal style, allow for variation in students' work on this activity sheet. The version in the Answer Key is just a suggested option.

Interrupted Quotations, page 105

Building on previous activities, this sheet adds the refinement of handling quotations that are interrupted by source words. To simplify this activity, ask students to read each item aloud before your students add the correct punctuation. Encourage readers to read each item silently before they read it to the class, since there are no punctuation marks to help them know where to pause or how long to pause. (There are, however, slightly bigger spaces between words where punctuation needs to be added. Add this hint for students who need extra help.)

More Than One Sentence, page 14

Before your students tackle this activity, remind them that the quotation for each different speaker gets its own paragraph. This rule often makes the lefthand margin look odd, as on this activity sheet, but it helps readers switch their minds to a new speaker.

For enrichment, put a dialogue passage on an overhead for your students. Choose a passage with one or more speakers saying more than one paragraph at a time. Use this activity to show that normal paragraph rules apply to quotations. To show that a speaker will continue to speak in the next paragraph, we don't use closing quotation marks at the end of a paragraph. The last paragraph of a speaker's turn in a conversation is the only one with both opening and closing quotation marks. The final marks signal the end of the entire quotation.

Indirect Questions, page 107

If this concept is new to your students, try some oral practice before they do this sheet. After you explain what direct and indirect questions are, toss out an indirect question and ask students to change it into a direct question. Once your students can translate these questions easily, give them direct questions to change into indirect questions.

If this activity sheet is difficult for your students, do it as a class and show the work on an overhead. Ask for different ways to turn each question into an indirect question, such as the following:

Where were you on June 22?

I wonder where you were on June 22.

I'd like to know where you were June 22.

Maybe you could tell me where you were on June 22.

I'll bet you could tell me where you were on June 22.

Titles of Short Works, page 108

Explain that a *work* is something produced by creative energy, such as a book, an opera, or a piece of art. The titles of most major works are italicized or underlined, as your students will see in the Italics (Underlining) unit in this book. Short works are usually parts of major works: "The Smelly Car" episode is part of the *Seinfeld* TV series.

100% Punctuation

Definitions in Sentences, page 109

Explain to your students that a word used as a word is italicized, as in the example here:

The word *gaga* means "foolish or crazy."

In handwritten work, underlining replaces italics.

The sentences in this activity are somewhat forced in order to give your students practice using quotation marks to set off definitions in sentences. Your students need to know and apply this rule, yet they need to use it cautiously. Too many quoted definitions can distract readers, interfering with their understanding of what they're reading.

Slang or Special Words, page 110

Caution your students against overusing this punctuation rule. The purpose of the rule is to offer a tool to warn readers they might need to stop to think about the quoted words, either because the words are likely to be unfamiliar or because the way the words are being used is uncommon or unique. Writers should avoid slang in formal writing. In general writing, there's no need to enclose common slang in quotation marks because most readers are familiar with it. It's also a good idea not to use quotation marks to make sure readers get the humor of a message, as with puns. Compare these examples:

Ned "fell" for Diana right away. He met her at his first ski lesson.

Ned fell for Diana right away. He met her at his first ski lesson.

It's usually funnier when readers discover the humor on their own.

Be cautious in proofing students' work on this activity. The story is loaded with slang or expressions that could meet the criteria for enclosing them in quotation marks, yet enclosing all of them would be overkill. If possible, put this activity on an overhead and do it with your whole group of students. The Answer Key gives one version. Accept other logical versions appropriately.

Quotation Within a Quotation, page 111

Remind your students that names of TV series and books are italicized, but names of show episodes are just enclosed in quotation marks. Also, students who are familiar with *zero hour* and *catch-22* will probably opt not to enclose these phrases with quotation marks, but students not familiar with these terms might prefer to set them off with quotation marks.

A Quotation As Part of a Sentence, page 112

The purpose of setting off parts of sentences that are actually someone else's words is to give writers a way to show which words came from some other source. Using quotation marks in these cases is less important than using quotation marks for all direct quotations. The key difference with a quotation that's part of a sentence is that the writer has incorporated someone else's words into an original sentence.

Proofreading, page 113

Direct your students to proof the Editor's Note as well as the story in this activity. To simplify this activity, ask your students to underline the source words for each quotation before they add the quotation marks.

100% Punctuation

Quotation Marks

Quiz

Rewrite these sentences. Add quotation marks where they belong. Some of these sentences also need commas to punctuate quotations correctly.

1. Tristan said I don't see anything so messy about my room.

2. This stuff on the floor and your desk Dad explained is what I'm talking about.

3. Then Dad told Tristan to clean his room before he did anything else.

4. Tristan found his guitar and played This Land Is Your Land a few times.

5. Then he called Joel and asked Want to shoot some baskets later?

6. Sure, let's do it! Joel said. What time will you be there?

7. As soon as I get released from cleaning prison Tristan said sarcastically.

8. While I wait for you, maybe I'll write a poem called Cleaning Blues Joel suggested.

100% Punctuation

Quotation Marks

Overview

Quotation marks signal the actual words someone said, the title of a short work, or something special about the words within quotation marks. Always use quotation marks in pairs, one set to open a quotation and one set to close it.

Gerta said, **"Marvin is such a great guy!"**

In this unit, you will learn about these ways to punctuate quotations:

- Direct quotations — Lauri said, **"Peas taste yucky."**

- Interrupted quotations — **"Peas,"** Lauri declared, **"taste yucky."**

- Indirect quotations — **Lauri said that peas taste yucky.**

- Titles of short works — Have you read **"Hot Dog"** by Shel Silverstein?

- Slang or special words — Little Tabitha calls potatoes **"day toes"** now.

- Definitions within sentences — The prefix *extra-* means **"outside or beyond."**

- Quotations within quotations — **"Have you heard the song 'Plunk Pond' by the Toads yet?"** Sean asked.

- Quotations as part of sentences — **"It is warm"** was the first sentence that Helen Keller ever spoke.

100% Punctuation   Copyright © 1998 LinguiSystems, Inc.

Quotation Marks

Direct Quotations

Use quotation marks to enclose the **direct quotation,** the words someone says. The words that tell who said the direct quotation and how they were spoken are called the **source words**. The direct quotation below is boldfaced. Notice the punctuation marks.

➡ Cleopatra commanded, **"Peel me a grape."**

Rewrite each sentence. Add quotation marks where they belong.

1. Why are you pounding so hard, boy? asked Captain Ahab.

2. Sir, I'm trying to close the hatch, replied young Abe.

3. Just use your hands to turn the handle! exclaimed the captain.

4. But, sir, it's stuck, Abe responded.

5. No way, just watch me, boy! yelled the captain.

6. Oof, ugh! grunted the captain as he tugged the handle.

7. Just pound that handle, boy! commanded the captain.

Quotation Marks

End Marks

Use the correct end mark to punctuate a quotation. The end mark of a sentence or a question always goes before the closing quotation marks.

➡ Ray asked, "Can you keep a secret?"

Margaret replied, "Of course I can."

Ray whispered, "Paul's middle name is Eggbert!"

Use a comma to replace a period when the source words follow a direct quotation. Compare the punctuation for the examples below with the ones above.

➡ "Can you keep a secret?" Ray asked.

"Of course I can," Margaret replied. *Changed the period to a comma.*

"Paul's middle name is Eggbert!" Ray whispered.

Add the correct end marks and quotation marks.

1. How long does it take to clean your room asked Mom

2. Brenda responded, Well, I have to read everything before I throw it away

3. Why don't you read it when you get it and then throw it away Mom suggested

4. You know, your brother's room is always so clean continued her mom

5. Brenda sighed, That's not fair

6. He's just a kid Brenda complained

7. Mom countered, I don't see what is so different between you and your brother

8. Is anybody home shouted Grandpa

9. We're over here in Brenda's pigpen answered Mom

10. Reminds me of your room when you were Brenda's age, Doris Grandpa chuckled

100% Punctuation

Quotation Marks

Interrupted Quotations

Sometimes a direct quotation is interrupted or divided by the source words. If the second part of an interrupted quotation starts a new sentence, capitalize the first word. If the second part finishes the sentence from the first part, don't capitalize the first word.

➡ "What," Tanya asked, "is hanging from your nose?"

"I don't know," Gus answered. "It might be a piece of spaghetti."

✎ Add the correct quotation marks, punctuation marks, and capital letters where they belong.

1. Even just a bus ride Mark lamented is an adventure with you

2. We have the police, the CIA, and the Royal Mounted Canadian Police looking for us Mark continued not to mention your former boyfriend

3. Mark, dear Leonetta purred it really isn't all that bad

4. Not all that bad roared Mark I don't see how it could get much worse

5. You may have started an international incident Mark pointed out just because you didn't want to sit next to a man who smelled like sauerkraut

6. But he did smell like sauerkraut Leonetta complained He really did

7. Yes, but did you have to take his container of sauerkraut off the bus asked Mark and walk into the waiting hands of drug police

8. How was I to know pleaded Leonetta that he had hidden illegal drugs in the smelly sauerkraut

9. I couldn't believe Leonetta pointed out that anyone would open that smelly container

10. I'm pretty sure Mark stated that the real smuggler agreed with you

100% Punctuation

Quotation Marks

More Than One Sentence

If a quotation has more than one sentence, use just one pair of quotation marks to enclose the whole quotation.

➡ Rose muttered, "Nobody picks up dirty clothes around here but me. I wish I had a dollar for every smelly sock or dirty T-shirt I've picked up this week. It's just not fair!"

If a quotation is interrupted, enclose each part of it in a pair of quotation marks.

➡ "Nobody picks up dirty clothes around here but me," muttered Rose. "I wish I had a dollar for every smelly sock or dirty T-shirt I've picked up this week. It's just not fair!"

Add quotation marks where they belong.

Hello, welcome to Quick Food. May I take your order? asked the cheery counter attendant.

Yes, I'll have a Value Meal 2, responded Matt.

Would you like fries with that? came the cheerful reply.

Don't fries come with a Value Meal 2? I mean, if I didn't want fries, Matt grumbled, I'd have ordered just a burger and a soft drink.

You don't have to be so grumpy! the attendant said, a bit less cheerfully.

Matt growled, Well, maybe I like being grumpy. Especially when I know what I'm ordering and I order it. Then when someone asks me a question she should know the answer to, I get even more grumpy. So are you happy now?

Sure, but if you'll look at the menu, the cheery counter attendant explained, you'll see that a Value Meal 2 comes with a choice of cole slaw or French fries. A value meal with cole slaw is a Value Meal 2a, and a value meal with French fries is a Value Meal 2b. So would you like fries with that? asked the cheerful counter attendant.

100% Punctuation

Quotation Marks

Indirect Questions

A direct question asks a question and ends with a question mark. An indirect question tells about a question, but it doesn't ask a question directly. Don't use a question mark at the end of an indirect question.

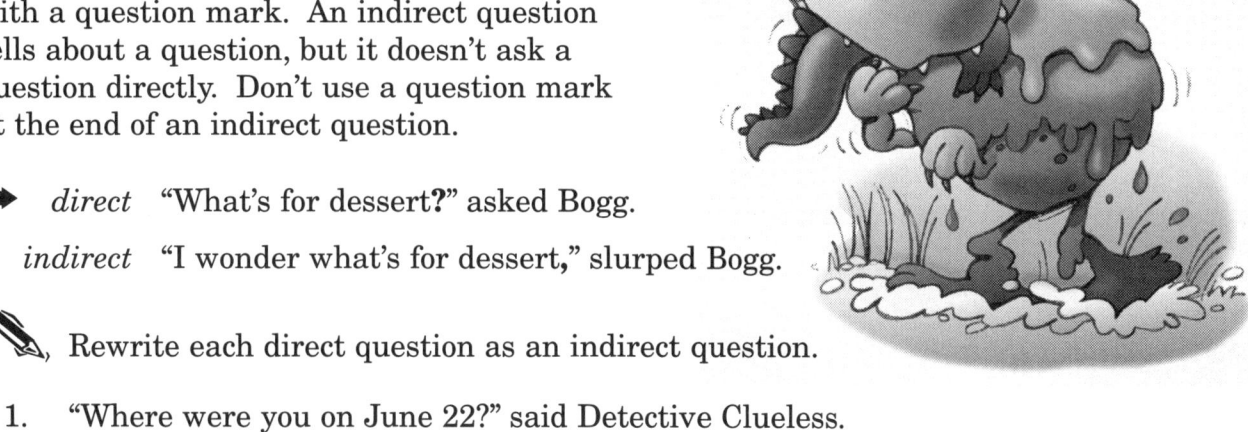

➡ *direct* "What's for dessert?" asked Bogg.

indirect "I wonder what's for dessert," slurped Bogg.

✎ Rewrite each direct question as an indirect question.

1. "Where were you on June 22?" said Detective Clueless.

2. "Do I have to tell the truth?" Bogg replied.

3. Detective Clueless responded, "Would you rather be arrested?"

4. Bogg replied, "Did you say 'digested'?"

5. "Is this a joke?" said Detective Clueless.

6. "Could I please have some fresh flies?" said Bogg hopefully.

7. "Don't you mean French fries?" Detective Clueless corrected.

8. "Slurp! Now who else has a question?" said Bogg.

100% Punctuation

Quotation Marks

Titles of Short Works

Enclose titles of short works in quotation marks. Short works are things like songs or writings shorter than a book, a movie, or a play. Here are some short works:

short poems	short stories	newspaper articles
songs	TV show episodes	magazine articles

Use quotation marks to enclose the names of short works in sentences.

➡ We sang "This Is My Country" for graduation last year.

✏ Add quotation marks where they belong.

Our band director says, "If it isn't a Sousa, it isn't a march!" I guess we'll be playing The Stars and Stripes Forever forever. We flute players would rather play show tunes like The Sound of Music. Our English teacher says that the movie based on the book *Gone with the Wind* inspired some great music. With our luck, all we'd get to play from that movie is Dixie.

Maybe our music teacher could arrange Sergeant Pepper's Lonely Hearts Club Band by the Beatles for us to play instead of Stars and Stripes Forever. We flute players have to work as hard as slaves, but we never get any respect.

Here comes the band director with our new piece, The 1812 Overture. I wonder how hard the flute part is in this one.

Quotation Marks

Definitions in Sentences

Use quotation marks to enclose definitions in sentences.

➥ The word *gaga* means "foolish or crazy."

✎ Add quotation marks where they belong.

1. In Yiddish, *nosh* means to eat a small snack.

2. A *haploid*, my dear Watson, is an organism with but half the normal number of chromosomes.

3. A *mesocarp* is the part of the cherry you eat between the pit and the skin.

4. Grandpa's favorite expression, *verbum sap*, means enough said.

5. The word *flout* means to treat with contemptuous disregard.

6. A *hat trick* means the scoring of three goals by a single hockey player in one game.

7. *Putsch* means a secretly plotted and suddenly executed attempt to overthrow a government.

8. A secondary verb meaning of *pestle* is to beat, pound, or pulverize with a pestle.

9. The word *spoonerism*, named after William A. Spooner, means a transposition of initial sounds of two or more words, such as *dig bait* for *big date*.

10. A *thaumaturgist* is defined as a performer of miracles.

Quotation Marks

Slang or Special Words

Use quotation marks to enclose unusual expressions, slang words, or technical words.

➡ That "thing-a-ma-bob" is actually a "thermonuclear recalculation heat duct temperature monitor."

✎ Add quotation marks where they belong.

On Starship 587, Elaine took a "sashay" along the space station's flight deck. Captain Hip Rune watched her on his monitors to protect the "li'l filly," as he called her. Hip liked to think of himself as a "man's man," stronger and smarter than any woman. He felt it was his duty to protect women, since they were clearly the "weaker sex." Actually, Elaine was about as fragile as a "pet rock," although Hip was clueless about her strength and her expertise.

Elaine, the station's first engineering officer, was the only one who knew the "Series 5 Acceleration Sequence," so Hip needed her. Hip hated needing some "sweet little thing" to run his manly space station. Besides, Hip was kind of "sweet on" Elaine. He'd just have to show her he was "top dog" so she'd have the proper respect for him.

Hip was daydreaming about Elaine when his elbow slipped and activated the "Intruder Alert" alarm. Elaine was halfway through her "Cadet Emergency Drill" before Hip knew there was a problem. He saw Elaine securing doors in the corridor outside his command post. Well, maybe he'd just have to "mozey on out" to visit with her. Surely she'd be impressed with his "to-die-for" aftershave.

Quotation Marks

Quotation Within a Quotation

Use single quotation marks to enclose a quotation within another quotation. Use the apostrophe key on a keyboard to create a single quotation mark.

➥ Jill said, "My mom used to read us the poem 'Hiawatha' when we were little."

"Next time," my teacher said, "don't use so many 'you know's' in your speech."

✎ Add single and double quotation marks where they belong.

1. Josh's teacher said, The excuse the dog ate my homework just won't work this time, Josh.

2. I can't believe you think I would use those weasel words, answered Josh. I'm much more creative than that!

3. Then just why is your report on the article Thousands Flee Flood not here? Ms. Lane demanded.

4. You see, the TV program *Nova*, which is totally educational, had a special on last night, Josh explained.

5. Josh continued, Their special, Flood of the Century, related directly to my report.

6. With her hands on her hips, Ms. Lane said, I don't care what you watched on TV last night. It's zero hour for your report.

7. Josh gave it one more try. He said, This is a real catch-22. I can't learn about the flood from TV, yet I'm supposed to write a report about it.

8. You're in luck, Josh, said Ms. Lane with a smile. You can sit down right now and show me what you learned from both the Thousands Flee Flood article and the Flood of the Century special.

100% Punctuation

Quotation Marks

Quotation As Part of a Sentence

Sometimes a sentence has a quotation without using any source words. The quotation is used as part of the sentence. When a quotation is blended into a sentence, follow these rules:

- Use quotation marks to enclose the quotation.
- Don't capitalize the first word of the quotation.
- Don't add a comma before or after the quotation.

➡ I agree with Davy Crockett. It's best to "be sure you're right, then go ahead."

✎ Add quotation marks where they belong.

1. Ask what you can do for your country has become part of pop culture.

2. Boy Scouts aren't the only ones with a be prepared approach.

3. I want you is said by more employers than just Uncle Sam.

4. The expression show me the money came from the movie *Jerry Maguire*.

5. The you break it, you buy it policy of Deedee's Gift Shop makes me nervous.

6. My sister always says she needs just a few minutes in the bathroom, but she hogs it for at least an hour every morning.

7. I hope you have an m'm, m'm, good day!

8. I never get tired of that song, so play it again, Sam.

9. Don't worry! It's only halftime, and it ain't over till it's over.

10. Mother Teresa helped people she called the poorest of the poor.

100% Punctuation

Quotation Marks

Proofreading

Add the correct punctuation and quotation marks where they belong.

"Avast, ye maties!" shouted Captain Bly.

"What does *avast* mean, anyway?" inquired Nate. "I mean, pirate guys are always swaggering around saying 'swabbies' and 'walk the plank' and stuff like that. What does it all mean, anyway?"

"That's true," commented Wil. "If any term is not in the dictionary, we should demand an explanation."

"What be ye maties gibberin' about?" asked Bly.

Editor's Note: As used here, *matie* means a crew member of a ship. *Maties* is the plural of *matie*. The language in this story is adapted from *Mutiny on the Bounty*, copies of which can be purchased at your local bookstore or checked out of your local library. Now back to our story.

"Ye made me forgit my place," complained Bly.

Wil said, "Yes, an editor can be a nuisance. But your place is not as our captain, Bly. You're more suited to be our cabin boy."

"That'll be 40 lashes for sassin'!" ordered Bly.

Nate responded, "Since Wil and I are the only two crew members, 'maties,' as you call us, how do you propose to carry out your order? Besides, since this ship is really a Sixteen Flags Themepark ride, why don't you knock off the British pirate routine?"

Colons

Teacher Guide

A colon comes after an independent clause, and it signals readers to pay attention to the explanation or other important information coming up. A colon also separates parts of conventional material, such as titles and subtitles or hours and minutes (2:15).

The most common error in colon usage is putting a colon after an incomplete sentence to introduce a list, as in this example:

Please bring: string, glue, and paper.

A colon follows only an independent clause:

Please bring the following: string, glue, and paper.

Enrichment Activities

- Write some sentences like these on the board:

    The following students will not have to take the test Marco, Zoe, Lee, and Shavonne.

    Meet me at 345.

    I'd like these pizza toppings salami, cheese, mushrooms, and onions.

    Ask your students to proofread these sentences for ease of reading. What suggestions do they have to make the sentences clearer? Guide them to using a colon to improve the readability of each sentence. Afterward, ask them to create additional examples, using these sentences as a base.

- Write these sentences on board:

    The ingredients are: milk, flour, sugar, and eggs.

    The ingredients are milk, flour, sugar, and eggs.

    These are the ingredients: milk, flour, sugar, and eggs.

Ask your students to identify the sentence that's punctuated incorrectly (the first one). Talk about the reason it's incorrect: A colon only follows an independent clause, a clause that can stand by itself as a complete sentence. Since this rule is often violated, ask your students to be colon cops for a week, watching for both correct and incorrect use of this punctuation mark. Post examples of colon usage on a bulletin board, identifying both correct and incorrect usage.

Activity Sheets

Overview, page 117

After reviewing this information with your students, help them find examples of colons used correctly in their textbooks or other handy reading materials.

Introducing Lists, pages 118 and 119

Remind your students before they begin page 118 that there aren't always determining words (such as *the following* or *as follows*) before a colon. Also, to simplify this task, have your students underline the items in the list in each sentence before they add the colon.

Since there is more than one correct way to revise each sentence on page 119, review your students' answers as a group. Encourage a variety of acceptable responses. The Answer Key lists just one alternative for each sentence; accept other appropriate answers as correct.

100% Punctuation

Long Quotations, page 120

In formal writing, most long quotations are indented so they are set off from the rest of the text. As with lists, the colon follows an independent clause.

incorrect   He said: "There should . . . ."

correct   He said these words: "There should . . . ."

Restatements or Explanations, page 121

Traditional grammar resources require the second independent clause in this type of sentence to begin with a capital letter. More current resources have dropped the need to capitalize the second clause. This book follows the current resources (no capital needed). The most important lesson here, though, is the use of the colon to join two sentences that are closely related in that the second explains or clarifies the first. The colon tells readers to think about the first sentence as they process the second.

Note that both colons and semicolons can join two independent clauses or sentences together. A sentence after a colon explains or clarifies the first sentence. A sentence after a semicolon offers a contrast or an additional thought to the first thought. The semicolon replaces a conjunction such as *and, but,* or *so*.

    I'm late for a good reason: I overslept.

    I'm usually on time; today, I'm late.

Business Letter Openings, page 123

Again, this activity features the traditional use of the colon. In practice, more and more business letter syle manuals advocate using a comma after the introduction rather than a colon. Use your own judgment in teaching this rule, sharing your own ideas about style.

Character Dialogue, page 124

Share some play scripts with your students to get their eyes used to colons in dialogue.

Groups of Numbers, page 125

Give your students practice in reading numbers with colons aloud. After they finish the activity sheet, write just the answers on the board. Ask students to read each one to the class.

Supplement this activity with some analogies, using the traditional analogy framework:

    hot:cold::loud:quiet

Have your students read each one aloud as "___ is to ___ as ___ is to ___."

Titles and Subtitles, page 126

For extra fun and practice, ask your students to create a fun title and subtitle for their own autobiography. Start the fun by sharing your own version.

Proofreading, page 127

Ask your students to read this story aloud to check their work here. Talk about the role of colons: to signal an upcoming explanation or clarification of a sentence.

Colons

Quiz

Rewrite each item. Add colons where they belong.

1. I think my first novel will be *Dating Don't Even Bother*.

2. I'd like to introduce the world champion maker of toe jam Ray Hunt.

3. Please bring these things on the field trip a jacket or sweater, a lunch, sunglasses, and a signed permission form.

4. We'll leave at 1030 sharp.

5. There's just one thing on my mind vacation.

6. Use a 3 1 ratio to mix the oil and vinegar.

7. The ingredients are as follows cooked rice, vinegar, oil, and chicken.

8. I have a huge problem I've lost my wallet.

100% Punctuation

Colons

Overview

A colon (:) means "pay attention to what follows." The information after a colon is often an addition or an explanation of the information before it.

The information before a colon is usually an independent clause (a clause that could be a whole sentence by itself).

> Aunt Bertha told me the ingredients for her special pancakes: 2 eggs, ½ cup milk, 2 cups of flour, and ¼ cup of melted butter.

In this unit, you will learn about using colons to signal these kinds of things:

- lists
  Here's what I want for my birthday: a ferret with a cage, ferret food, and some ferret toys.

- long quotations
  About the poor, Mother Teresa said: "Let us not be satisfied with just giving money. Money is not enough. They need your hearts to love them."

- restatements or explanations
  Scamp is a great dog: he's always happy to see me.

- some appositives
  Most people don't know Mother Teresa's given name: Ganxhe Agnes Bojaxhiu.

- business letter openings
  Dear Sir:

- character dialogue
  Hamlet: To be or not to be, that is the question.

- groups of numbers
  We left at 11:15.

- between titles and subtitles
  Dreams: Making Them Come True

100% Punctuation

Colons

Introducing Lists

An **independent clause** can stand alone as a complete sentence. When you add a list to an independent clause, use a colon after the clause to tell readers a list is coming next.

➡ *independent clause*   I have three things to trade.   *list*   a giant water pistol
a slingshot
my sister's diary

altogether   I have three things to trade: a giant water pistol, a slingshot, and my sister's diary.

An independent clause before a list often ends with **determining words**, such as *the following*, *as follows*, *for example*, or *below*. Use a colon after these words to signal the list that follows.

➡   The rules are **as follows:** no shouting, no pushing, and no cheating.

✏ Add colons where they belong.

1. What we have here is a complete mix-up no grounds to complain, no violation of any law, and no obvious way to recover.

2. We have experienced the following misunderstanding, confusion, and danger.

3. To get out of danger, our needs are as follows a plan, someone to execute the plan, and enough money to fund the plan.

4. We used to have everything the people, the money, the plans, and the energy.

5. Look what I just found plans, spare parts, and fuel!

6. Let's divide into three teams home base, transport group, and forward base.

7. Home base will be responsible for three areas scheduling shipments, receiving shipments, and repairing vehicles.

8. The transport group will control voyage-specific tasks operating the shuttle craft, recording outgoing inventories, and recording incoming inventories.

9. Forward base will be responsible for outer space maneuvers dockings, landings, explorations, and takeoffs.

Colons

Introducing Lists

Here's a tricky part about using a colon to introduce a list. DO use a colon after an independent clause, words that could stand alone as a sentence. DON'T use a colon after a verb or a preposition.

➥ *incorrect*   The foods I like are: tacos, apples, and anchovies.
               Marco is afraid of: thunder, snakes, and marshmallows.

     correct   The foods I like are as follows: tacos, apples, and anchovies.
               Marco is afraid of three things: thunder, snakes, and marshmallows.

Rewrite each sentence to correct the colon errors.

1. We all need reassurance, understanding, and encouragement.

2. Many of you are looking for a home, a career, and a friendship.

3. You should put aside your fears, questions, and thoughts.

4. Without thinking, follow your heart, emotions, and feelings.

5. I will lead you to places you haven't been, things you haven't seen, and wonders you never imagined.

6. My enemies are rational thought, critical thinking, and independent reasoning.

7. Just follow TV, radio, and magazines without thinking for yourself.

8. That way, the media will control your present, your future, and your life.

100% Punctuation

Colons

Long Quotations

Use a comma to set off a short quotation. Use a colon to set off a long quotation, especially in formal writing.

➤ *short quotation*   Jacques Cousteau said**,** "When a person takes his first dive, he is born to another world."

   long quotation   Jacques Cousteau said**:** "I'm now fighting for my own species. I finally understand that we ourselves are in danger. The notion of sustainable economic development ... is impossible; it's an illusion. Our Western model is not valid for a world of limited resources."

Add commas and colons where they belong.

1. The United States Constitution, written in 1787, begins "We the People...."
2. Abraham Lincoln said in his Gettysburg Address "Fourscore and seven years ago, our forefathers brought forth upon this continent a new nation, conceived in liberty and dedicated to the proposition that all men are created equal."
3. In 1776, the United States Declaration of Independence justified revolution with these words "We hold these truths to be self-evident, that all men are created equal, that they are endowed by their Creator with certain unalienable Rights, that among these are Life, Liberty and the pursuit of Happiness. That to secure these rights, Governments are instituted among Men, deriving their just powers from the consent of the governed. That whenever any form of Government becomes destructive of these ends, it is the Right of the People to alter or to abolish it and to institute a new Government, laying its foundation on such principles and organizing its powers in such form, as to them shall seem most likely to effect their Safety and Happiness."
4. During the French Revolution on August 26, 1789, the Declaration of the Rights of Man and of the Citizen was adopted. In Article 4, it says "Liberty consists in being able to do anything that does not harm others...."
5. The United Nations Universal Declaration of Human Rights adopted in 1948 says "All human beings are born free and equal in dignity and rights. They are endowed with reason and conscience and should act towards one another in a spirit of brotherhood."

100% Punctuation

Colons

Restatements or Explanations

When a second independent clause restates or explains the first independent clause, use a colon to separate the clauses.

➥ Aunt Dot is a clumsy waitress: she's always dropping things.

✎ Add colons where they belong.

1. Our teacher said we cannot have any problems today the principal is visiting our classroom.

2. This is our big chance the teacher can't yell at us with the principal around.

3. We each have a plan I'm going to try something special.

4. We will all do something that way the teacher can't pick on just one person.

5. We are all excited we have never planned something together before.

6. It is our big morning we're all going into the classroom.

7. The principal is clueless he'll never know what hit him.

8. Class, please pay attention the principal wants to say a few words to us.

9. He is giving us the reason for his visit he thinks teachers don't use enough strict discipline.

10. We'd better change our plans we don't want to let our teacher show how strict he can be.

100% Punctuation

Colons

Appositives

An **appositive** is a word or phrase that renames or explains a noun or pronoun in a sentence. Think of an appositive as "a positive clue" that describes something. The appositives are underlined in the sentences below:

➡ Pretzel, <u>our dog</u>, sheds hair everywhere. *our dog = Pretzel*

When you want to emphasize an appositive that comes after an independent clause, use a colon to separate it from the first clause.

➡ There is only one thing to do: <u>apologize</u>. *apologize = thing to do*

I've discovered the perfect pillow: <u>my cat</u>. *my cat = perfect pillow*

Add colons where they belong.

1. Uncle Jason is a brick someone you can always count on.

2. That's what we're laughing at your drawing.

3. That's what I'm worried about sneezing without a tissue.

4. Dad writes a cartoon strip under a secret pen name O. Well.

5. That's my biggest problem sweaty hands.

6. Trudy finally got what she asked for privacy.

7. On the floor below the desk was the best evidence candy wrappers.

8. I'm glad about one thing no homework for two weeks.

9. My goal for this year is simple graduate.

10. I knew it was a bad day when the most feared substitute walked in Ms. Furrchin.

11. My neighbor invented the greatest toy ever a Whizbo.

12. Share one of life's greatest treasures with others your cheery smile.

Colons

Business Letter Openings

In a formal letter or a business letter, use a colon after the salutation.

➡ Dear Sir: Dear Madam: To Whom It May Concern:

For each item below, write a salutation to begin a letter. Use a comma after the salutation if it's an informal letter. Use a colon after the salutation if it's a formal letter.

1. Your uncle sent you a birthday present.

   Salutation _____

2. You want to order an audiotape from the Super Duper Sounds Company.

   Salutation _____

3. You want your city council to change a law about in-line skating on sidewalks.

   Salutation _____

4. You are away from home. You want to write to your sister.

   Salutation _____

5. You want to write to your best friend, who is staying with relatives for a month.

   Salutation _____

6. You want the Jenkins Library to open earlier in the mornings.

   Salutation _____

7. You want a copy of an article from the *Gazette Press*.

   Salutation _____

8. You want to apply for a job at the Green Grocery Store.

   Salutation _____

Colons

Character Dialogue

In a script for a show, use a colon after a character's name to signal that the words ahead are spoken by that character.

➡ Buster: Want to see what I can do with my tongue?

Tanya: No way! Go find a mirror and entertain yourself.

✎ Add colons where they belong in this script.

1. Stan What do you call a worm on a razor blade?
2. Oliver I don't know, what do you call a worm on a razor blade?
3. Stan A cutup!
4. Oliver That's awful.
5. Stan Why are worms the best workers you can hire?
6. Oliver I wouldn't have any idea.
7. Stan Because worms work dirt cheap!
8. Oliver I'm leaving if you don't stop.
9. Stan Why do you see worms on sidewalks when it rains?
10. Oliver I don't care!
11. Stan Because you look!
12. Oliver I can't take it any longer!
13. Stan What's worse than finding a worm in your apple?
14. Oliver Help!
15. Stan Finding half a worm!
16. Oliver That's it, I'm cracking up.
17. Stan What should you do if you find worms in your bed?
18. Oliver Augggghhhhh!
19. Stan Sleep somewhere else!
20. Oliver How can I worm my way out of this script?

100% Punctuation

Colons

Groups of Numbers

Use a colon to separate certain kinds of numbers so they are easier to read.

➡ *hour and minutes*   It is now **3:15** P.M.   *It is now three-fifteen P.M.*

Bible chapter and verse   Genesis **2:14**   *Book of Genesis, Chapter 2, Verse 14*

proportions   Mix milk with flour **2:1**.   *Use 2 parts of milk to 1 part flour.*

lines from plays or poems   Hamlet **I:2:10**   *Hamlet, Act I, Scene 2, Line 10*

Rewrite each item using colons to show parts or divisions.

1. twelve-thirty P.M. _____

2. one forty-five A.M. _____

3. three parts vinegar to 1 part baking soda _____

4. Act IV, Scene 2, Line 43 _____

5. Psalm 100, Verse 1 _____

6. three twenty-three P.M. _____

7. A is to B as C is to D. _____

8. volume 12, page 1011 _____

9. 2 minutes and 34 seconds _____

10. one forty-five A.M. _____

100% Punctuation

Colons

Titles and Subtitles

Some books have a main title and a subtitle. The subtitle usually adds information to explain more about the main title or the content of the book. Use a colon to separate a title from a subtitle.

➡ title *Nostril Tricks*

subtitle *Ten Ways to Disgust Your Friends*

Name the author of *Nostril Tricks: Ten Ways to Disgust Your Friends.*

✎ Here is a list of new publications from Gross Publishing. Add a colon to separate each title from its subtitle.

1. *Projectile Vomiting Five Easy Lessons*

2. *Ripped Underwear Frankie the Ferret Shares His Tricks*

3. *Headlock Tips How to Survive Close Contact with Armpits*

4. *Acne Agony Why You Shouldn't Pop Pimples*

5. *Open-Mouth Chewing Why No One Will Eat with You*

6. *Nose Hygiene Taming Unruly Nose Hairs*

7. *Toe Jam Is Not Your Friend How to Keep Your Feet Healthy*

8. *Belching Elocution How to Talk on Burps*

9. *Bug Patrol How to Check Yourself for Lice*

10. *Asking for Trouble Why Tapeworms and Leeches Make Poor Pets*

11. *Gross but True How the Sweatshirt Got Its Name*

12. *Green Sleeves An Alternative to Tissues*

100% Punctuation

Colons

Proofreading

Add colons where they belong.

My name is Sergeant Thursday. I wear a badge. I wear a uniform, too I don't want you to get the wrong idea. Anyway, I'd like to tell you about something incredible the story of a crime in the West Side.

It was 12:05 A.M., and I was working the night watch. My partner, Sydney, had just come back from the delicatessen with these goodies a salami sandwich, a large soft drink, fries, and an apple pie. I asked him, "Sydney, how can you eat that stuff? It's bad for you."

Sidney replied by quoting the Surgeon General "The recommended daily allowance of carbohydrates includes some grams from each of the food groups. When a diet restricts the intake of calories, the patient's metabolism slows down and becomes more efficient. Therefore less food is needed to produce energy, and weight loss is not obtained."

That's when the call came in the call that began our mystery. It was about a robbery over in the West Side. When we got there, they had already collected the following clues an old shoe, a coat hanger, a chewed dog bone, a rawhide strip, and a Maltese falcon. That's when we came up with the title of the book we would write about this caper *The Maltese Dog's Falcon The Night the Chew Toys Got Loose.*

Semicolons

Teacher Guide

There are two major functions of the semicolon:

1. joining independent clauses that are closely related

2. separating items in a series when any items themselves have commas

A semicolon is a stronger punctuation mark than a comma, but weaker than a period. When we read, we pause slightly longer for a semicolon than we do for a comma.

Enrichment Activities

- To illustrate the usefulness of the semicolon in joining thoughts together, write this sentence on the board:

    You can lead a horse to water you can't make it drink.

    Have your students talk about what this sentence means. Then help them make the meaning clearer by adding a semicolon between the two independent clauses. Your students might suggest adding the word *but* between clauses, making the meaning crystal clear. Show them that a semicolon can take the place of *but*; write both versions of the sentence on the board.

- To illustrate the function of the semicolon in separating lists when one or more items contain a comma, write this sentence on the board:

    At the pet store, we held a ferret, which was only two weeks old, two Siamese kittens, which looked identical, and a boa constrictor, which had a huge bulge of food it was digesting.

Ask volunteers to read the sentence aloud. Then ask your students how they could improve the readability of this sentence. Guide them to add semicolons between the items of the list.

Activity Sheets

Overview, page 131

Explain that most sentences that are joined by a semicolon could just as well be two separate sentences. The only reason to link them into one sentence is to show readers that the ideas expressed in these sentences are more closely related than the ideas in most other sentences. The second idea can be closely related to the first because it adds key information, tells a consequence, or offers a direct contrast to the first idea:

It's awfully hot; I'm thirsty. *addition*

It's hot; I'm getting a drink. *consequence*

It's hot outside; it's cool inside. *contrast*

Once your students understand this use of the semicolon, review the use of the colon to join independent clauses. Help your students differentiate the correct use of the colon, to precede an explanation or clarification of the first sentence, from the correct use of the semicolon, described above. Use these examples to show the difference:

I'm late for a good reason: our bus was in an accident. *The second clause explains the reason mentioned in the first clause.*

Our bus was in an accident; I'm late. *The second clause tells a consequence of the first clause. The semicolon takes the place of* so *or* and.

100% Punctuation

Separating Independent Clauses, pages 132 and 133

Proof the activity on page 132 as a group. Encourage students to explain their rationale for using or not using a semicolon to join particular independent clauses. The Answer Key gives one acceptable version of the story. Accept appropriate alternative versions.

The activity on page 133 highlights the use of the semicolon before an introductory expression that begins the second clause. Two abbreviations often serve the same purpose as the introductory expressions listed in the example box on this page: *e.g.* which means "for example" and *i.e.* which means "that is." Teach your students about these abbreviations as you cover this material.

A comma is required after some of these introductory expressions, including *that is, for example, for instance, e.g., i.e., in other words, on the other hand,* and usually *however*. This comma is optional with the other expressions. For simplicity, we chose to use the comma after each introductory expression in this activity.

To demonstrate that changing the position of an introductory expression like these doesn't change the need for a semicolon between the independent clauses, write these sentences on the board:

Mike finished his test early; nevertheless, he stayed until the bell rang.

Mike finished his test early; he stayed, nevertheless, until the bell rang.

Mike finished his test early; he stayed until the bell rang, nevertheless.

In a List or Series, page 134

It might help some of your students to draw lines between each complete item in a series to determine where to put semicolons. If none of the items has a comma in it, there's no need to use a semicolon between items. If even one item has a comma in it, a semicolon must separate each item in the series.

Proofreading, page 135

This activity requires students to apply what they've learned about commas, colons, and semicolons. Suggest that your students read their revised sentences aloud to proof them. Also, some students might find it easier to rewrite the items on a separate sheet of paper than to change the punctuation on the page as is.

100% Punctuation

Semicolons

Quiz

Add semicolons where they belong.

1. It's almost time for lunch I'll save my snack for later.

2. Sofia can really keep a secret I always open my big mouth.

3. Our Quiz Whiz team includes Jake, who knows everything Rhonda, a total brain Bob, who doesn't know the time of day and yours truly.

4. I was hoping to sit beside Doug today however, he's absent.

5. We wrote letters to the mayors of Shreveport, Louisiana Raleigh, North Carolina and Tulsa, Oklahoma.

7. I ran here as fast as I could I hope I'm not too late.

8. Weather can affect your mood for instance, lots of people feel blue on a rainy day.

9. Some people think a rabbit's foot is lucky rabbits might disagree.

10. Please turn that music down otherwise, no one can hear my great speech.

11. I thought my puppy was a mutt in fact, it's a border collie.

12. The game is almost over, so let's leave besides, it's about to rain.

13. We walked all the way to Chelsea's apartment meanwhile, Beth took the bus.

14. I can't decide whether my favorite season is fall, when the leaves turn bright colors winter, when snow covers the ground spring, when everything is green and new or summer, when the days are long and warm.

Semicolons

Overview

A semicolon (;) signals a major division in a sentence. It is a stronger punctuation mark than a comma, but not as strong as a colon or a period. When you read, pause slightly longer for a semicolon than for a comma, but not as long as for a period.

A semicolon also avoids confusion when there are commas in a sentence.

➡ I have relatives in Peoria, Illinois; Erie, Pennsylvania; and Taos, New Mexico.

It would be nice to live closer together; then, I could get to know my cousins.

In this unit, you will learn about using semicolons to do these things:

- separate independent clauses that are closely related

    Kerry is great at keeping a secret; I'm not.

    Ian drank his soda too fast; he burped for about ten minutes.

- introduce words that signal explanations or examples

    Troy has lots of allergies; for example, he's allergic to homework.

- separate items in a list or a series if at least one of the items has a comma

    I'd like you to meet Paul, my brother; Toby, my neighbor; and Widget, my new beagle puppy.

100% Punctuation

Semicolons

Separating Independent Clauses

An independent clause can be a sentence by itself. You can also combine independent clauses to make one sentence. You can use a coordinating conjunction (*and, or, nor, for, but,* or *so*) between the independent clauses. If the independent clauses are closely related, you can use a semicolon between them instead of a coordinating conjunction.

➡ *separate sentences*   I told the truth. Jake did, too.
combined with coordinating conjunction   I told the truth, **and** Jake did, too.
combined with semicolon   I told the truth**;** Jake did, too.

Most of the time, writers use coordinating conjunctions to combine independent clauses. Substitute a semicolon for a coordinating conjunction only when you want to show a strong, dramatic connection between the two clauses.

Rewrite each sentence on another sheet of paper. Use a semicolon to replace each coordinating conjunction between independent clauses.

1. The band concert was over, and now they couldn't stop giggling.

2. They went to a local restaurant, but how could they read the menu when they couldn't stop laughing?

3. The waiter couldn't speak English very well, but he began laughing with them anyway.

4. The girls asked some embarrassing questions, and the boys blushed.

5. They didn't answer, so the girls asked once again.

6. The waiter showed up at the table again, and he heard the question.

7. Now the girls blushed, and they began laughing nervously.

8. From the next table, we tried to hear what they said, but we couldn't hear it.

100% Punctuation

Semicolons

Separating Independent Clauses

Sometimes the second independent clause in a sentence is introduced with a word or phrase that signals the relationship between the two clauses. The most common of these expressions are listed in the box below.

for example	that is	consequently	therefore	however
for instance	besides	accordingly	otherwise	furthermore
as a result	in fact	in addition	meanwhile	in other words
afterwards	also	moreover	finally	on the other hand

Use a semicolon before these expressions and a comma after the introductory expression.

➡ Charlie surprised a skunk; <u>consequently</u>, Charlie smelled terrible.

Add semicolons and commas where they belong.

1. It was football day therefore Hank needed his lucky shirt.
2. They never lost a game when he had his shirt as a result all of his teammates made sure he wore it.
3. Today he couldn't find the shirt in other words they were doomed.
4. Bobbie Brown, his offensive line leader, told him not to forget the shirt however the shirt was nowhere to be found.
5. Hank frantically looked for the shirt meanwhile the team waited for him.
6. Hank found a shirt that looked almost like his lucky shirt consequently he might be able to fool everyone.
7. He couldn't find his lucky shirt on the other hand this substitute shirt might work.
8. He had to try it besides a shirt won't win or lose a game.
9. After the game, everyone said Hank's play played a major part in their win in fact they had never seen him play better.
10. The team was ecstatic with the win however the players still wanted Hank to find his lucky shirt.

Semicolons

In a List or Series

If the items in a list or a series have commas in them, use a semicolon to separate each item instead of a comma. Using semicolons avoids confusion for readers.

➡ At Thanksgiving dinner, we enjoyed seeing Uncle Mac, who has six fingers on one hand; Uncle Theo, who parts his hair below one ear and sweeps it over his bald head; and Aunt Trudy, who doesn't gush over us and pinch our cheeks.

✏ Add semicolons and commas where they belong.

1. Nikki's ideal man would be someone who would not be afraid to show emotions of happiness love or fear who would be considerate enough to remember holidays birthdays and special occasions and who would spend a lot of money time and attention on her.

2. Josh wore baggy pants with a drawstring belt plaid pattern and wide cuffs a shirt with puffy sleeves plastic pearl buttons and a starched collar and black shoes with wingtips leather soles and platform heels.

3. Nikki's friends couldn't believe that Josh a boring nerd was Nikki's friend that Nikki a sharp dresser would be seen with Josh a fashion misfit and that together a totally opposite couple they could find things in common.

4. All things considered everyone concluded that Nikki an intelligent woman would make up her own mind that Josh a somewhat responsible person would show his true colors and that her friends if they wanted to remain friends would have to become friends with Josh.

Semicolons

Proofreading

Proofread these sentencess. Correct any punctuation errors you find.

1. In the mall we stopped at the Sugar Cane which sells; fresh candies nuts and dried fruits, The Athlete's Foot which has sweatshirts banners and T-shirts for most teams, and McDoogals where we had burgers fries and milk shakes.

2. My favorite characters in the movie were: Fang, a vampire, Doofus, the detective's dog, and Harry Furrball, a werewolf.

3. Dripping with sweat; Brian walked toward the stage to give his speech.

4. Although the teachers have no contract; they decided to keep working.

5. We have everything we need for a great picnic; lemonade sandwiches, homemade brownies games, and a blanket.

6. Lester doesn't have a clue about manners, for example he chews with his mouth open and uses his arm to wipe his mouth instead of a napkin.

7. I'm not supposed to eat chocolate: I eat it anyway.

8. Take Jason with you because; he wants to go, besides, you promised; you would let him come, with you.

9. Many people wear clean underwear every day: I'm not one of them.

Hyphens

Teacher Guide

A hyphen is a handy tool to separate words, parts of words, or numbers. Unlike periods, commas, colons, and semicolons, a hyphen doesn't signal readers to pause for any amount of time. Hyphens are strictly visual tools.

Enrichment Activities

- Designate a bulletin board to hyphens for a week or two. Ask your students to bring in as many examples of print with hyphens as they can. To get them started, make a class list of all the uses of hyphens your students can think of, including things such as hyphenated last names, phone numbers, and locker combinations.

- This unit presents traditional hyphen rules, but your students will readily see these rules ignored in informal writing, especially in marketing copy for commercials and brand names. Since hyphen usage isn't the only grammar or punctuation area advertisers routinely adapt for marketing purposes, talk about the reasons ads sometimes change the rules. Which changes can your students spot? What do they think about those changes?

Activity Sheets

Overview, page 139

In addition to the hyphen rules in the overview box, point out that we use hyphens between letters to indicate a word being spelled:

Damon is spelled D-a-m-o-n.

Encourage your students to use a dictionary whenever they're uncertain about hyphenating words.

Syllable Division, page 140

Fortunately, many word-processing programs today include automatic hyphenating. These programs usually avoid leaving only two letters on a second line and so forth. Still, your students need to know when to override such programs and where to break words in handwriting.

If you have a preferred style of hyphenating words for your assignments, share it with your students.

Compound Numbers, page 141

For enrichment, have your students do some practice work on the board about writing checks. Explain typical check information, especially the two ways we write the amount of each check:

$32.43

Thirty-Two and 43/100————

Prefixes and Suffixes, page 141

The key to mastering hyphens with prefixes and suffixes is to use a dictionary if you have even the slightest doubt. Many words with the prefix *re-* are now blended into one word, except where a hyphen prevents reading confusion, such as *resign* vs. *re-sign*. This type of confusion is addressed in the activity on page 146.

Before your students do this activity, write these words on the board so everyone is familiar with the correct form:

half brother, half sister
stepbrother, stepsister, stepdad

100% Punctuation

Compound Adjectives, pages 143 and 144

The purpose of linking multi-word adjectives before a noun is to chunk them in the reader's mind. Note these examples:

> He's a one of a kind dog.
> He's a one-of-a-kind dog.

The entire string of words functions as a one-word adjective describing *dog*. Here are some common compound adjectives to share with your students:

> the out-and-out winner
> a dog-eat-dog world
> a do-it-yourself project
> a pie-in-the-sky attitude
> anti-wrinkle cream

See how many other examples your students can add to this list.

Fractions, page 145

Generally, if a preposition follows a fraction, the fraction is being used as a noun, so it isn't hyphenated:

> two thirds of a glass
> two-thirds full

Preventing Misreading, page 146

Encourage your students to read the words in this activity aloud to help them decide the difference a hyphen makes in pronunciation or readability. A dictionary is the best resource whenever there is any confusion about whether to hyphenate or not.

Proofreading, page 147

Alert your students that two of the items in this activity don't need any hyphens.

100% Punctuation

Hyphens

Quiz

Add hyphens where they belong.

1. John F. Kennedy was the thirty fifth President of the U.S.

2. When the cookies are three fourths baked, sprinkle them with sugar.

3. Mice are the best selling pets in the pet store.

4. I can't eat highly spiced food, so I'll have a twice baked potato, please.

5. Most people are anti pollution, but not enough people are pro active about it.

6. One half of our class walks to school and one third takes a bus.

7. *My Life As an Ex Child* is a hilariously funny book by a well known author.

8. Soldiers honored the veteran with a twenty one gun salute at his funeral.

9. Marcia is highly honored to be president elect for the birdwatchers' club.

10. Uncle Leo is more well known for his off color jokes than for his athletic ability.

11. They're building a six story apartment where the run down stores used to be.

12. The new anti drug campaign got off to a first rate start today.

13. Leon finished the race in one hundred forty first place for all runners, but twenty second place for his age group.

14. Have you tasted that smoke cured ham with the honey mustard sauce?

15. I'd love to have a half time job with full time pay, wouldn't you?

Hyphens

Overview

Hyphens connect certain words or parts of words together.

- c-a-t
- twenty-one-gun salute
- well-known author
- self-respect
- r o c k - b o t t o m
- a half-hour's walk

In this unit, you will learn these ways to use hyphens:

- Dividing a word at the end of a line to keep the righthand margin even

    I've always wanted to be an **astro-naut**, but I get dizzy in an airplane.

- Connecting parts of compound numbers

    twenty-two, thirty-nine

- Connecting some prefixes and suffixes

    ex-con, president-**elect**

- Connecting some multi-word adjectives

    We live in a **five-story** apartment.

- Connecting fractions used as adjectives

    The law passed by a **two-thirds** majority.

- Avoiding confusion

    They **re-entered** the building.

100% Punctuation

Hyphens

Syllable Division

When a word is too long to fit at the end of a line, use a hyphen to divide the word into two parts. Put the first part of the word at the end of the line, and add a hyphen to show the word will continue on the next line. Then put the rest of the word at the beginning of the next line. Here are some rules to help you divide a word at the end of a line:

1. Don't divide a one-syllable word. — lounge, dream, wealth
2. Divide a word with double consonants between the double consonants. — bub-ble, lit-tle, pep-per
3. Divide a word after a prefix or before a suffix. — dis-miss, anti-human, human-ity
4. Don't put a single letter at the end of a line. — elim-inate, *not* e-liminate
5. Don't begin a line with only two letters. — perma-nently, *not* permanent-ly
6. If a word already has a hyphen, divide it where the hyphen is. — self-control, father-in-law

Use the rules to divide each word as though it's at the end of a line. There may be more than one way to divide some words correctly.

1. troublesome _____
2. battle _____
3. immediately _____
4. continuing _____
5. excitable _____
6. exaggeration _____
7. mosquito _____
8. incredible _____
9. anonymous _____
10. subcategory _____
11. mannerism _____
12. explanation _____
13. proofreading _____
14. exclamation _____
15. investigate _____
16. nonclassified _____

Hyphens

Compound Numbers

Use a hyphen between each part of compound numbers from *twenty-one* to *ninety-nine*.

➥ 36   thirty-six   184   one hundred eighty-four

✎ Rewrite each item using words instead of numbers. Use hyphens appropriately.

1. Carla ate 49 jellybeans and 21 licorice dots.

2. I've watched 75 episodes of *Seinfeld* reruns.

3. Aunt Dee lives at 159 Oak Street.

4. Which state was the 41st to join the United States?

5. Nutty Flakes have 132 calories per serving.

6. Do you get Channel 28 where you live?

7. Bake it for 45 minutes at 325 degrees.

8. Nelson gained 27 pounds last summer.

9. My dog weighs 72 pounds.

Hyphens

Prefixes and Suffixes

Use a hyphen between the prefixes *all-*, *self-*, and *ex-* and root words.

➡ all-knowing　　　　self-image　　　　ex-patriot

Use a hyphen between a prefix and a proper noun or a proper adjective.

➡ pro-Chicago Bears　　　non-Canadian　　　anti-Martian

Add hyphens where they are appropriate.

1. Dale was Lisa's mother's ex brother-in-law.

2. Did that make him her ex uncle?

3. In the pre divorce world, he was her uncle.

4. Now that it is post divorce, is he her nothing?

5. Her most important question was this: Do you get presents from an ex uncle?

6. She would ask her all knowing stepbrother, Jeremy.

7. Having already had two mothers, her half brother was the most anti divorce person she knew.

8. Jeremy said that he might actually be her ex stepbrother, since her mom was not his mom, and his dad was not her dad anymore.

9. Therefore, Jeremy's dad was Lisa's ex stepdad.

10. Lisa decided that, if her mother ever remarried, she would be her mom's self appointed marriage preserver.

100% Punctuation

Hyphens

Compound Adjectives

Sometimes two or more adjectives are connected with a hyphen because they act like one adjective modifying a noun.

➡ a **three-year-old** girl   a **black-and-white** cat   a **ten-mile** ride

Hyphenate a compound adjective if it comes before the noun it modifies. If it comes after the noun, don't hyphenate it.

➡ a **well-known** author   an author who is **well known**.

If the first word in a two-word modifier is an **-ly** adverb, don't hyphenate the modifier.

➡ a **slightly wet** sneeze   a **swiftly** moving car   a **highly** spiced taco

✎ Add hyphens where they belong.

1. It was a little known fact that Otto was the world's greatest runner.

2. In fact, no one but Otto knew this closely guarded secret.

3. Today was the all important, first race of what would be his wildly successful career.

4. At the end of today, he would have an undefeated, one race career.

5. Otto was running what used to be the one mile race that was now a 1,500 meter run.

6. The 1,500 meter run was still a fairly difficult, middle distance race.

7. Otto had super long cleats on his track shoes for extra traction.

8. His lightning fast start would swiftly propel him into the front runners.

9. Otto wore a blood red jersey and cobalt blue shorts, since those were his school's colors.

10. As Otto came to the starting line, he could see a half lap stagger for each lane.

11. The starter's gun went off; it was time for Otto to begin his world famous career.

100% Punctuation

Hyphens

Compound Adjectives

When compound adjectives are in a series, use a hyphen and a comma after each element in the series. Use the word after the hyphen only once.

➡ **Two-, three-, four-,** and **five-window** <u>tents</u> are on display.

Use a hyphen to join compound adjectives with a numeral at the first element.

➡ We're taking a **3-mile** <u>walk</u> to the park today. We took a **two-mile** <u>walk</u> yesterday.

✎ Add hyphens where they belong.

1. Have you ever had 24 hour flu that lasted 36 hours or more?

2. I need 6, 12, 18, and 24 inch rulers for my art project.

3. There was a five car collision on our street last night.

4. Why does the military give a 21 gun salute sometimes?

5. Uncle George took an eight hour dose of cough medicine.

6. There were two, three, and four alarm fires in Chicago last week.

7. I caught a 20 second peek at my sister's two year diary.

8. We have four, six, and seven story buildings in our apartment complex.

9. My three and four year old nieces are coming to visit.

10. This fan has a four way switch.

11. I need 24 and 36 exposure films, please.

12. Brian broke his record in the 200 meter run and the twenty yard dash.

100% Punctuation

Hyphens

Fractions

Hyphenate a fraction that modifies a noun. Don't hyphenate a fraction that is used as a noun itself.

➡ **Two thirds** of the students voted for Ned.   *used as a noun, the subject*

Ned won with a **two-thirds** majority.   *used as an adjective modifying a noun*

Add hyphens where they belong.

1. One half of the test will be math story problems.

2. That is more than one half trouble: that is huge trouble for students like me.

3. If a glass is one third full, and it holds twelve ounces, how many ounces are in it?

4. If there are 12 people, and two fifths of them are blond, how many are blond?

5. How can there be four fifths of a blond person?

6. Can a person be four ninths alive?

7. If a glass is one half full, can it be one half empty at the same time?

8. If John takes Sally for a ride in the country, and if his gas tank is one tenth full, is John an honorable person?

9. The team concentrated seven tenths on the game and three tenths on the crowd.

10. Pretzel is one half collie and one half black labrador.

11. One fourth of the students in our class has an older brother.

12. The track meet was two thirds over before we won an event.

100% Punctuation

Hyphens

Preventing Misreading

Use hyphens to avoid awkward letter combinations that might confuse readers. With some words, a hyphen changes the meaning of a word.

➥ **recollect** — to remember   **re-collect** — to collect again

With other words, a hyphen signals readers how to pronounce syllables.

➥ **semiicy** — *confusing to read*   **semi-icy** — *easier to read*

Match these words to the definitions on the right. Write the letters in the blanks.

1. ____ re-sign   a. to dye again
2. ____ resign   b. to count again
3. ____ coop   c. late night or overnight
4. ____ co-op   d. to quit from a job
5. ____ red-eye   e. a group that works together
6. ____ redye   f. a cage for poultry
7. ____ recount   g. to sign again
8. ____ re-count   h. to tell again

Rewrite each word. Add a hyphen if the word needs it to avoid confusing readers. Use a dictionary to check your work.

1. antiintellectual   _____
2. hydroski   _____
3. semiinvalid   _____
4. uncalledfor   _____
5. preengineered   _____
6. microorganism   _____
7. agegroup   _____
8. antiinflammatory   _____

100% Punctuation   Copyright © 1998 LinguiSystems, Inc.

Hyphens

Proofreading

Add hyphens where they belong.

1. The pitcher was two thirds full before it cracked into twenty two pieces.

2. Melissa is anti desserts these days so she can wear her all time favorite jeans.

3. Let's go for just a half hour ride before we re enter the data for our project.

4. Uncle Mike has a ten year old motorcycle in absolutely perfect condition.

5. The taste of our cafeteria food is highly overrated.

6. How loud is a twenty one gun salute?

7. Call me at one thirty this afternoon, before I start my new part time job.

8. I'll take the eighty two bus to Thirty Second Avenue.

9. Neil never thought he'd win a weight lifting competition.

10. Rodrigo, a well known bullfighter, is an ex citizen of Spain.

11. Rodrigo is more well known in Mexico now than in Spain.

12. Four and five year old children have class in the all purpose room.

13. Dad is one half English, one quarter Chinese, and one quarter Jamaican.

14. Save fifty five percent at our going out of business sale!

15. If our landlord won't be pro pet, he could at least be pro cat or pro dog.

Italics/Underlining

Teacher Guide

Italics, or underlining in handwritten material, call attention to certain kinds of information. The most common use of italics is for titles of major works, such as books, movies, magazines, or works of art. We also italicize the names of certain vehicles, foreign words unfamiliar to most readers, and words or letters referred to as words or letters.

Using italics to show emphasis or emotion is acceptable in some situations, but not generally recommended. It is usually better to reword a passage to convey the meaning or emotions to readers.

Enrichment Activities

- Distribute newspapers or magazines to small groups of students. Have them find as many examples of italicized print as they can. As each group shares its findings with the class, ask the students to guess the reason for the italics in each case. Use these reasons to start a list of situations requiring italics.

- For extra practice in italicizing TV series and enclosing episodes in quotation marks, ask your students to keep a log of all TV shows they watch for one week. Have them exchange lists for proofreading of punctuation.

Activity Sheets

Overview, page 151

Be sure your students know that underlining in handwriting replaces italics in print. If your students word process their work, make sure they know how to use the italics function of their software program.

Titles, pages 152-154

Before your students begin these pages, take time to list examples of each type of major work listed in the box on page 152.

Also, ask your students which makes a stronger visual impact on readers, quotation marks or italics. They can look at the examples on page 152 to form an opinion. In general, italics call more attention to themselves than quotation marks. That's why the more important information, the name of an entire major work, is in italics and a part of that work is enclosed in quotation marks.

Review general title capitalization rules with your students as they do these pages, too. For example, the words *a, an,* or *the* are not capitalized or italicized as the first word in a title unless they are part of the actual title themselves:

> Have you read the *Wall Street Journal*?
> Have you read *The Giver*?

For enrichment, bring in some pictures of works of art. Let your students select their favorite five pieces and write a short statement about each one. Ask them to include the title of the piece in each statement so they get practice in italicizing or underlining these titles.

The story on page 154 deals with the future. Since the spacecraft titles will be unfamiliar to them, read the story to them before they begin their work. To simplify this activity, point out that names of spacecraft should be underlined, but the name of a moon base is

100% Punctuation

like the name of an airport and doesn't need to be italicized or underlined.

Foreign Words, page 155

As diverse a population as we have, there are regional differences in familiarity with words and sayings from non-English languages. In some areas, for example, *mano a mano* is readily said and understood; in other areas, that expression is rare and could be italicized as an unfamiliar expression. Teach your students to use their own judgment in deciding which non-English words or expressions to underline or italicize. When in doubt, of course, your students should consult a dictionary.

Another alternative is to ask five or six people what the expression in question means. If everyone is familiar with the expression, chances are it doesn't merit being italicized or underlined if the writing is for local readers.

Words, Letters, or Numbers As Such, page 156

This activity should help your students understand the reason for italicizing words, letters, or numbers used as such. Some of the items are open to initial confusion without the visual clue of italics. For example, the word *power* in item four could be misread as *word power* without the help of italics:

> That linebacker really put some pow in the word power when he hit me.

> That linebacker really put some pow in the word *power* when he hit me.

Emphasis, page 157

Encourage a volunteer to read this fun story, exaggerating each italicized word. For contrast, have another volunteer read it without any emphasis on the italicized words. What could the author's purpose be in italicizing all those words? What impact does it have on the readers and listeners?

Caution your students to avoid using italics for emphasis in formal writing. It is best left for comic effect in casual writing.

Proofreading, page 158

You might want to review this vocabulary before your students tackle this proofreading activity:

> trawler — a small fishing boat
> tawdry — cheap or gaudy
> Cotton Mather — a Pilgrim clergyman and author

Italics/Underlining

Quiz

Add underlining to show which words should be italicized.

1. The <u>Queen Elizabeth II</u> is cruising the Atlantic this month.

2. Did you see the rerun of "Cold Feet" on <u>Mad About You</u> this week?

3. I'm not into piercing toes or kneecaps, but <u>chacun à son gout</u>, I always say.

4. How do you spell <u>judgment</u>, with or without an <u>e</u> in the middle?

5. An article in the <u>Wall Street Journal</u> explained the rising cost of paper.

6. My favorite novel is <u>The Giver</u> by Lois Lowry.

7. Some people think the number <u>13</u> is unlucky; I think they're right.

8. The painter Georgia O'Keeffe had a way of making even animal bones beautiful and graceful, as in her <u>Summer Days</u> painting.

9. Oil shale has layers of <u>kerogen</u>, a waxy material made of decayed matter.

10. I think <u>however</u> is the most boring word in our language.

11. Have you read <u>Catherine, Called Birdy</u> yet?

12. Aunt Rosie named her new plane <u>Herby 2</u>.

13. After watching the movie <u>Apollo 13</u>, I'm not sure I'd like to be an astronaut.

Italics/Underlining

Overview

Italics or underlining help writers emphasize things like certain titles and special uses of words. Use italics where they're needed when you type or word process your work. When you handwrite, use underlining instead of italics.

➡ My favorite poetry book is *Falling Up* by Shel Silverstein.

My favorite poetry book is Falling Up by Shel Silverstein. (handwritten, with Falling Up underlined)

Use italics or underlining to highlight titles of major works. Use quotation marks to highlight shorter works or parts of major works.

➡ Do you remember the sharp-toothed snail in the poem "Warning" from *Where the Sidewalk Ends*?

In this unit, you'll learn about using italics (or underlining) to call attention to these kinds of things:

- **Titles of major works** — books, movies, plays, operas, TV series, magazines, comic strips, and computer software
  - *Romeo and Juliet*   *Wheel of Fortune*
  - *TIME*   *TV Guide*
  - *Windows 95*   *Garfield*

- **Titles of works of art** — paintings, statues, sculptures
  - *Mona Lisa*   *Statue of Liberty*
  - *The Scream*   *The Thinker*

- **Names of certain vehicles** — specific ships, trains, aircraft, and spacecraft
  - *Titanic*   *Mir*
  - *Apollo 13*   *Zephyr*

- **Foreign words** — unfamiliar, non-English words
  - *vita nuova* (Italian for "new life")
  - *en ami* (French for "as a friend")

- **Words, letters, or numbers referred to as such**
  - I got a *B* on my math test.
  - *The* is the most common English word.

- **Words that need special emphasis**
  - I said it was due *yesterday*.
  - Don't even *think* about calling me again.

100% Punctuation 151 Copyright © 1998 LinguiSystems, Inc.

Italics/Underlining

Titles

Use italics or underlining to set off the titles of major works. Types of major works are listed in the box. To set off the titles of parts of these major works, use quotation marks. Don't capitalize *a*, *an*, or *the* in front of a title unless the word is part of the actual title.

books	magazines
movies	newspapers
operas	comic strips
plays	long poems
TV series	radio programs
journals	computer software

➡ Let's watch the rerun of "Fun with Dick and Janet" on *3rd Rock from the Sun*.

I just read "The Danger of Sleeping Pills" in the *Reader's Digest*.

✏ Underline the titles of major works. Add quotation marks around the titles of parts of major works.

1. Chapter 3, Watermelon Seed Spitting, is the most important lesson in the book How to Be an Annoying Guest.

2. We can't wait for the final episode, Mary Goes to Fargo, on The Restless Ones.

3. Everyone listens to Truck Talk on our public radio station.

4. The Wall Street Journal doesn't have Beatle Bailey or any other comic strips.

5. You can't be an Italian-American if you don't know The Marriage of Figaro from The Barber of Seville.

6. The shortest chapter of the shortest book is Games to Play on Rainy Days from The Sahara Nomad's Guide to Watersports.

7. Even though Vivian Leigh didn't realize it, the song Dixie was around long before the movie Gone with the Wind.

8. Let's play Doom on Jason's new 856 platinum-plus, macro-media computer.

9. They reviewed the 856 platinum-plus, macro-media computer in the latest issue of Computing Today.

100% Punctuation

Italics/Underlining

Titles

Italicize or underline the titles of works of art, including paintings, statues, and sculptures. Don't italicize or underline the words *a, an,* or *the* at the beginning of a title unless the word is part of the actual title.

➡ Edvard Munch painted *The Scream* in 1893.

I love the colors in the *Water Lilies* painting by Monet.

✎ Underline the titles of works of art.

1. What makes the smile in the Mona Lisa painting so interesting?

2. How old was Michelangelo when he sculpted David?

3. Goya's painting The Family of Charles IV is in a Spanish art museum.

4. Renoir captured the emotion and spray of the ocean in The Wave.

5. We like Claude Monet's The Grainstack (Sunset), even though it's just a haystack.

6. I wonder who created the Dying Warrior from the Temple at Aegina in 490 B.C.

7. Bird in Space is a 54" bronze piece completed in 1919 by Constantin Brancusi.

8. Henry Moore made stone look soft in his Recumbent Figure from 1938.

9. The Bride by Marcel Duchamp (1912) looks more like a factory to me than a bride.

10. I like Paul Klee's Twittering Machine, a whimsical piece in watercolor and ink.

11. How many dots are there in Side Show by Georges Seurat?

Italics/Underlining

Titles

Italicize or underline the titles of specific ships, trains, aircraft, and spacecraft.

➡ The *Titanic* was built to be the safest ocean ship in the world.

✎ Add underlining where it is needed to show titles.

    Captain San Holo left Club Far Out and piloted the Freedom Falcon through space. He was making the first trip to the Earth's moon since the Apollo 45 had landed on that lifeless asteroid. On the moon, Captain Holo would rendezvous with the Liberty II ship. The Freedom Falcon and the Liberty II were going to be retrofitted at Morton Moon Base. They would get new thrustors, stabilizers, and gyroscopes that would make them the equal of any Empire cruiser, even the awesome, quad-fire Maureen O'Banion IV.

    As Captain Holo approached the moon base, he was third in line behind the Lightning Cruiser and the Liberty IV. It would be a longer layover than he had expected; perhaps he would have time to visit Princess Kwani on the Venus IX ship.

Italics/Underlining

Foreign Words

Italicize or underline uncommon foreign words and expressions. Don't italicize or underline foreign words or expressions that most English speakers already know and understand. If a word is listed as a regular entry in most English dictionaries, you probably don't need to italicize it.

➡ George Washington was our *pater patriae*.   *Pater patriae* is Latin for "father of his country."

Would you like more pasta?   The word *pasta* is familiar to most English speakers.)

Use a dictionary to help you write the meaning of each word or expression. Then underline the words or expressions that are unfamiliar to most English speakers.

1. tout à fait _____

2. piñata _____

3. pour rire _____

4. nicht wahr? _____

5. mano a mano _____

6. karate _____

7. tempus fugit _____

8. jurisprudence _____

9. joss _____

10. che sarà, sarà _____

11. lingua franca _____

Italics/Underlining

Words, Letters, or Numbers As Such

Use italics or underlining to highlight words, letters, or numbers referred to as such. The easiest way to explain this rule is with examples:

➡ The number *42* was written above the name *Benson*.

How many *i*'s are there in your aunt's last name?

✎ Add underlining for words, letters, or numbers referred to as such.

1. It was the biggest game of the season. When the coach sent in the play split right, 65 left, on three, I thought it was 56 left.

2. I missed my block, got hit by the linebacker, and only remember the doctor asking, "Don't you even see the big E on top of the chart?"

3. I couldn't even remember if my name was spelled with one or two L's.

4. That linebacker really put some pow in the word power when he hit me.

5. After that play, I figured I should change my jersey number from 26 to 18 or some other number people wouldn't recognize.

6. I heard my friends outside in the hall say, "Here he is, room 655. Unless he thought the 6 was a 5, then it would be room 566."

7. I would never live this down. And what about the word live, anyway?

8. Spelled backwords, the word is evil; that's what my friends would do to me.

9. Just then our coach breezed in and said, "Lloyd, there's only one word for your play that saved the day: brilliant!"

Italics/Underlining

Emphasis

Sometimes writers use italics or underlining to emphasize words. Notice the difference in what these sentences mean:

➥ We *have* to leave now.   We have to *leave* now.   We have to leave *now*.

Try not to use italics for emphasis very often, especially in formal writing. It's usually better to rephrase your words so the italics aren't necessary.

Just for fun, here's some practice in reading material with italicized words. Read this story to a friend. Make sure you emphasize the italicized words.

I can't *believe* the teacher wants us to dissect a *live frog!* That is a positively *asinine* assignment. First, frogs are *unbelievably* slimey. Second, frogs live in the *mud!* Lastly, the mud probably smells *terrible*.

"By the way," Kevin helpfully chimed in, "when we slice open the live frogs, their blood and guts will *squirt out* all *over* the place!" That can't *be!* That is *totally* impossible. The frogs can *not* be *alive!* This has to be a violation of my Constitutional rights.

The teacher just walked in with seven *dead* frogs preserved in formaldehyde. That's better: not *much* better, but *better* nonetheless.

100% Punctuation

Italics/Underlining

Proofreading

Add underlining where it belongs.

Lois was always name dropping and saying, "Our family came over on the *Mayflower*." She made me feel like saying, "Yes, well, our family came over on the trawler USS *Tawdry*."

On TV tonight, we're supposed to watch "Courageous Beginnings," an episode of *Our American Heritage*. If it has anything to do with Pilgrims, Plymouth Rock, or Cotton Mather, Lois will use the opportunity to tell us again that her family has a reproduction of the painting *Pilgrims' Landing*, which shows her great-great-great-great grandparents.

Nona says her family came over on the ice bridge across the Bering Straight way before even Columbus and his *Niña*, *Pinta*, and *Santa Maria*. Now, that's what I call being first! But Mom says I should take Nona and Lois *cum grano salis*.* *C'est la vie*, we will just have to live with her. Here's the issue of *TV Guide*. Let me see when *Our American Heritage* starts. Oh, my gosh! It's three hours long! This had better be mighty entertaining!

**Cum grano salis is Latin for "with a grain of salt."

100% Punctuation

Answer Key

Capitals

Quiz, page 12

1. Every time I eat strawberries, I get a rash.
2. "After lunch," Dad said, "we'll see the Brooklyn Bridge and the Statue of Liberty."
3. When the Civil War started, both the North and the South thought they could win.
4. Our mayor wants everyone to agree not to smoke in the downtown area.
5. Was Abraham Lincoln the first President of the United States?
6. My mom said she could drive me to my interview with Mayor Johnson.
7. Is Venus the farthest planet from the Earth?
8. The title of the book I read is *Darth Strikes Again*.
9. Which dressing do you like better, Italian or French?
10. I hope we have lunch at Aunt Julie's house again.
11. Ms. Cohen, principal of our school, will retire at the end of this year.
12. Have you met Uncle George before?
13. My sister loves Mexican restaurants.
14. Have you ever read *Drums of the Jungle* by Tar Zahn?

Pronoun *I*, page 14

1. Patrick Henry said, "I have just begun to fight."
2. Martin Luther King said, "I have a dream."
3. Bart promised, "I will not use my sleeve to blow my nose any more."
4. Rhett Butler said, "Frankly, my dear, I don't care."
5. Vanessa said, "Just ask for me, and I will be there to help you."
6. James said, "Anything you can do, I can do better."
7. Mary asked, "Does anyone mind if I leave early today?"
8. As she played peek-a-boo with the baby, Jim's mom said, "I see you!"
9. After winning the race, Tonio said, "I am worn out, but I am proud!"
10. Uncle Sam said, "I want you."

Pronoun *I* and First Words in Sentences, page 15

1. I am an animal.
2. People say I'm a wild dog.
3. I am very smart and very loyal to the other animals in my pack.
4. My jaws are sharp and I run very fast on my toes.
5. I use my voice to howl or scare other animals away.
6. I can also use my ears, my hair, and my body to communicate.
7. My sense of smell is awesome!
8. If I meet a member of my pack that is more powerful than I am, I roll onto my back so we won't fight each other.

What am I? a wolf

Names of People, Pets, and Characters, page 16

In Joey's neighborhood, everybody has a special name, like Joey the Fish. How did Joey the Fish get his name? The neighbors all agreed that Joey ought to take showers more often. That's how Joey the Fish earned his name. Even Joey's dog, Spot, has a special name: Spot Full of Slobber. Teresa with the Eyes is known for making eyes at all the boys. Alex Pass 'Em All Checkov is the driver's license bureau examiner. Harry the Slip Connors can hide from anyone. Manny the Pickpocket is in jail for a while. Tony Fairway Riso is always on the golf course. Double Dribble Dale never could get the hang of playing basketball. What would your name be in Joey's neighborhood?

Titles, page 17

1. Officer Bronski gave a parking ticket to one of Sister Ann's nuns in Big City.
2. (no correction needed)
3. The nun asked the mayor, Willy B. Elected, to cancel the ticket
4. Mayro Elected told the nun she must obey the law while she did good works.
5. (no correction needed)
6. (no correction needed)
7. So Mayor Willy B. Elected gave Sister Ann's nuns special parking permits.
8. (no correction needed)
9. Officer Bronski, the mayor, the nuns, and the people of Big City were pleased.
10. (no correction needed)

Titles of VIP's, page 18

1. Woodrow Wilson was the 28th President of the United States.
2. The President's leadership brought the U.S. out of isolation in 1917.
3. Under Prime Minister Sir Robert Laird Borden, Canada had entered World War I three years earlier.
4. World War I started when Austrian Archduke Francis Ferdinand was shot in 1914.
5. When Germany marched across Belgium to get to France, the British Prime Minister urged Great Britain to declare war on Germany.
6. In the U.S., President Wilson tried to keep his country out of the war.
7. Canada's close relationship with Great Britain made it more difficult for her Prime Minister.

Relatives, page 19

Sally was spending the summer with her dad and Aunt Pam. Her aunt's house in the country was always fun to visit. Today was the day her dad had promised to take her fishing. Sally wasn't too keen on fishing, but she wanted to spend as much time as she could with her dad.

When her dad came downstairs, Sally was pleased that his tackle box was closed. At least the smelly, wriggly, slimy worms would be under cover. When they reached Aunt Pam's fishing hole, Sally was surprised that it was a pretty clearing along the bank of a stream. It would be a great place for a picnic, but a horrible place for hooking worms.

"It's time to bait the hooks," Dad said. Sally forced herself to look interested as her dad opened the tackle box. Inside the box were pretty lures in all kinds of colors with beads and feathery things attached. Sally's father noticed her surprise and relief. Her dad explained, "No serious fisherman uses worms anymore." Fishing was going to be fun after all, as long as Sally didn't have to clean any fish!

Brand Names, page 20

Jim couldn't help it, he was a national-brand-name kind of guy. He used Redken® on his hair, wore Levi® jeans and ate McDonalds'® fast food. Jim would wear any brand of shoes, as long as it was endorsed by a National Basketball Association player. He was the same way about beverages. He would drink Gatorade®, but he wouldn't drink the milk from the local dairy, Martha's Farm. If Coca-Cola® bottled Martha's Farm's dairy milk, that would be different. If Martha's Farm had cool T-shirts or a fancy Madison Avenue ad campaign to market it, Jim might consider drinking their milk. What really makes Jim's mom mad is that Jim's grandmother, Martha, owns Martha's Farm.

Geographic Names, page 21

Last year, my family went on vacation out West. We saw the Hoover Dam, the Grand Canyon, the Colorado River, and my sister's braces every time she smiled. Our first stop was Mount Rushmore in South Dakota. It was kind of cool seeing the Presidents carved in stone. A bee stung my sister in Custer State Park. She screamed, and a herd of buffalo stampeded after her. Then we headed up into the Rocky Mountains. Pike's Peak was so high, my sister got a nosebleed. In Yellowstone National Park, bears smashed my sister's camera. All in all, I'd say it was a great vacation!

Historic Periods and Special Events, page 22

My Uncle Vinny isn't married, and my mom thinks that's a good thing. He never dates the same woman for very long. Last New Year's Day, he came over with a list of possible Valentine's Day presents for the woman he was seeing. Mom was not impressed. She told Uncle Vinny that anyone he was seeing in January would not be around in February. Uncle Vinny looked hurt. He said that sometimes he went out with the same woman for more than two months. Just last year, he took the same woman to the Fourth of July fireworks that he had taken to the Memorial Day picnic in May. My mom pointed out that he was with a different woman by Labor Day in September. Uncle Vinny says he's just a modern man who should have been born in the Age of Romance. Mom thinks the Stone Age might be more fitting.

Books, Movies, Songs, and Shows, page 23

1. *A Wrinkle in Time*
2. *Ralph the Rascal*
3. *My Name Is Bozo*
4. *Taking It Easy*
5. *A Tale of Two Malls*
6. *Grody Gertrude*
7. *Max Is Missing*
8. *Mighty Fine Dreams*
9. *Is Anyone at Home?*
10. *Wind Beneath My Wings*

Adjectives from Names, page 24

1. Canadian bacon
2. plaster of Paris/paris
3. Cheddar/cheddar cheese
4. Roman numeral
5. Southern hospitality
6. Swiss cheese
7. French/french fries
8. Italian dressing
9. Mexican restaurant
10. Turkish bath
11. American habit
12. African violet
13. Dutch oven
14. German measles
15. Russian dressing
16. Indian summer
17. Japanese beetle
18. Labrador retriever
19. Arabian stallion
20. Irish setter
21. Mackinaw trout
22. Manila/manila paper
23. morocco leather
24. Roquefort cheese
25. Rosetta stone
26. Gouda cheese

Groups of People, page 25

Yesterday, we went to the International Food Fair at Jackson High School. There was great food everywhere, and lots of it! Ben tried Chinese pot stickers and Vietnamese fish balls. Beth raved about Amish Dutch apple-crumb pie. Leon and Pat shared a Greek gyro with a special sauce. Lavonne thought the Mexican hot chocolate was the best she'd ever had. Matthew complained that all the food was gross, especially Jamaican fried bananas. No one paid

100% Punctuation

any attention to him, though, because he's such a picky eater.

I can't decide which food was my favorite. It sure wasn't the French snails with garlic! The Hungarian goulash was pretty tasty, so I got the recipe for it. I guess the food I liked the best was Japanese sushi. It was not only delicious, but also beautiful with many different colors and patterns. Actually, it was as much fun to watch the chefs make it as it was to eat it!

Dates and Addresses, page 26

I can't wait for Friday, June 12, the beginning of summer vacation! I will be going to my dad's house in Chicago, Illinois. Most of the time I live with my mom in Peoria, Illinois. A lot of my friends are in Peoria, but I have friends in Chicago, also. We go to museums, shows, and the zoo when I visit my dad over the summer. It is great to see the Chicago Art Institute, Adler Planetarium, and the Museum of Science and Industry. On the other hand, by the time I've spent two months with my dad, I miss my mom. When August 20 comes along, I'll be ready to head back to good old Peoria, Illinois.

First Words in Quotations, page 27

1. Troy asked, "Has anyone seen my comb?"
2. Angie whispered, "Someone with red hair and freckles has a crush on you."
3. "Class, please take out your math books," said Ms. Chang.
4. "There are pretzels on the counter for snacks today," announced Mr. Harvey.
5. Chad wondered, "Why does Aunt Flo look like she has measles?"
6. The announcer shouted, "Order your special alligator pencil today and save!"
7. "Golly, we haven't solved any crimes yet today," sighed Batboy.
8. "Don't worry, the Joker will be back soon," Bobbin said.
9. "Is anyone interested in seeing my coin collection?" Horace asked.
10. "You've grown at least an inch!" squealed Aunt Rachel.
11. Leroy asked, "Whose bright idea was it to climb this tree?"
12. Coach Nevins said, "Take a ten-minute break, team."
13. "How does this can opener work?" Josie inquired.
14. "Next time, check for a hole in your pocket before you put money in it," said Megan.
15. Jenny said, "Never make a bet about how many worms you can eat."

Interrupted Quotations, page 28

"Just the facts, ma'am," said Sergeant Joe Monday. "Tell me just the facts."

"Well, when we saw the car coming," Mrs. Nonetoobright said, "we thought there would be trouble."

"What kind of trouble, Mrs. Nonetoobright?" asked Joe Monday. "What kind of trouble?"

"The kind of trouble," she continued, "that I don't want any part of."

"That's pretty vague, Mrs. Nonetoobright," said the sergeant. "Can you be more specific?"

"The car was driving way too fast, and it was," she recalled, "much bigger than most of the other cars in the neighborhood. I didn't want to know anything about it or who was in it."

"Why is that?" asked Monday.

"If I knew too much," she volunteered, "then I'd have to get involved."

"What's wrong," asked Monday, "with being involved?"

"I knew if I got involved," continued Nonetoobright, "some police people were bound to come around and ask a lot of questions."

Letter Openings and Closings, page 29

1. Dear Hungry Pirate:
   Very truly yours,
2. Dear Aunt Nita,
   Sincerely,
3. Dear Paul,
   Very truly yours,
4. Dear Mom,
   Your son,

Abbreviations of Names and Places, page 30

1. Collections, Ltd.
2. Orlando, FL
3. P.O. Box 42
4. Gen. Grant
5. Ms. Louise Snodgrass
6. N.Y.C.P.D.
7. St. Louis
8. Frick and Frack, Assoc.
9. N. Tonawanda, NY
10. 354 NW St.
11. Bismarck, ND

Acronyms and Initializations, page 31

1. APB
2. COD
3. TGIF
4. RIP
5. AIDS
6. MADD
7. VCR
8. IOU
9. ASAP
10. NASA
11. ETA
12. POW
13. RSVP
14. ESP
15. BYOB
16. MVP

Special Things, page 32

Joan and Henry both go to Hilton High School in Brooklyn. They sit together in English Literature B and in math. Last Friday, Joan and Henry went on a date. They took the ferry to Staten Island. The ferry wasn't as fancy as the *Queen Elizabeth*, but they had a lot of fun.

Henry said he'd call Joan, but two days have gone by and there hasn't been any phone call! Joan hopes Henry doesn't expect a gold medal for promptness. She figures that she'll go to the track meet on

100% Punctuation

Wednesday. Henry will be running the two-mile relay. If he wants to be her Prince Charming, he'd better talk with her then. Otherwise, he'll be ancient history as far as Joan's concerned!

Proofreading, page 33

If a situation wasn't life threatening, it wasn't interesting enough for Nick Danger. "I like my situations hot," Nick always said, "and my Coca-Cola® cold."

Once, Nick was in the jungle by the Sao Francisco River in Brazil. He was traveling with native Indian guides. The President of Brazil was depending on Nick to bring him important information. Nick and his guides were traveling by boat through water thick with piranhas. Suddenly, the boat struck a boulder. Nick's Indian guides figured they were goners. Not Nick!

"Grab the sides of the boat," Nick shouted, "and hold them together!" Nick was no Superman, but he did command his guides' respect. They obeyed Nick, now their fearless leader. They paddled to the shore before the boat broke up.

The President of Brazil had given him up for lost when Nick arrived at the meeting of the National Congress. "Sorry I'm late, folks," Nick said, "but my boat sprang a leak on the way over."

End Marks

Quiz, page 36

1. .
2. . or !
3. ?
4. .
5. . or !
6. ?
7. ?
8. ?
9. . or !
10. .
11. ?
12. . or !
13. !
14. .
15. . or !
16. ?
17. !
18. .
19. . or !

Periods, page 38

At home, I have to eat my vegetables before I can get dessert. I don't see what the big deal is about vegetables. My mom says that they are good for me. If they are good for me, I wonder why they don't taste good. *Good* should go with *good*. If something tastes good, it should be good for you. My mom says it just doesn't work that way. Besides, she is the one who brings home the desserts. Since she has the desserts, I have to do what she tells me.

I wonder if we could get a dog that likes vegetables. We could train it to sit by the table. Then the dog could eat a carrot or some spinach if it fell on the floor. Then we could eat more desserts.

Question Marks, page 39

1. What is the meaning of life?
2. What is the answer to the ultimate question?
3. Douglas Adams in the *Hitchhiker's Guide to the Galaxy* said the answer is 42.
4. If the answer is 42, what was the ultimate question?
5. I don't know why anyone wants to remember what six times seven is.
6. Why don't things fall up?
7. Which came first, the chicken or the egg?
8. When you go to the store, be sure you get the right change.
9. If no one is around to hear it, does a tree falling make a sound?
10. When you can't see it, does it exist?
11. If you can answer these questions, you're a philosopher.
12. If you don't care, that's reasonably normal.

Direct and Indirect Questions, page 40

1. I wonder how long it will take to build that new building at the end of our street.
2. How did they figure out how much lumber they'll need?
3. I wonder how many new families will move in.
4. Is the building going to have a store in it?
5. Who would know how many workers will be building it?
6. I'd like to know how they keep all the workers busy.
7. When will it be finished?
8. I wonder how we'll know when the first people move in.
9. What if they have too much stuff to fit into their apartment?
10. Dad asked if I'd like to be a building engineer.
11. I wonder if I would like to build buildings.
12. How will I know unless I try it for myself?

Exclamation Points, page 41

I heard that our school will have uniforms next year. That's gross! Who says students all want to look alike? I don't understand how wearing uniforms helps students get a better education. Lots of students already get good grades. Wearing uniforms won't help kids study any better. What about the kids who drop out of school? Wearing uniforms won't make kids want to stay in school longer. It might even make some kids drop out earlier. Requiring uniforms is a crazy idea! We should encourage students to help each other learn, not to dress alike. If you agree, please come to Room 102 to sign a student petition against uniforms. We need your help!

Proofreading, page 42

Nedra couldn't think of the answer to the first test question. She wondered how she would pass this history test. She decided to skip the first question and go on to the next one. Oh, no, she couldn't think of the answer for the second question either! What was wrong? Why couldn't she think of any of the answers?

100% Punctuation

Nedra remembered how hard she had studied for this test. She had read the chapter three times. She had taken good notes. She practiced test questions with her stepmom and with her dad. Last night, she knew all the answers. Maybe what Nedra needed to do was take a deep breath and calm down.

Nedra closed her eyes. She took several deep breaths. Then she opened her eyes and read the first question again. It worked! She knew the answer right away. Nedra wondered why she had let herself get so uptight. After all, it was just one history test and she had studied for it. Nedra decided she would keep herself calm before she started the next test. Then the test would seem much easier right from the start.

Apostrophes

Quiz, page 46

1. Everyone's sure you're the teacher's pet.
2. That's why you got all A's this year.
3. It's anyone's guess why I don't get better grades.
4. I've been bustin' my bones this year.
5. It's hard to study at home 'cause it's so noisy.
6. Dorie's and Sam's friends are always coming over.
7. I'd like it quiet by seven o'clock every night.
8. Something's bound to change my luck soon.

Contractions, page 48

1. isn't
2. aren't
3. wasn't
4. weren't
5. hasn't
6. haven't
7. hadn't
8. doesn't
9. don't
10. didn't
11. can't
12. couldn't
13. wouldn't
14. shouldn't
15. mustn't
   won't

Contractions, page 49

1. I'm
2. He's
3. I'm
4. he'll
5. it's
6. he'll
7. it'll
8. It's
9. I've
10. that's

Contractions, page 50

'Twas the biggest night of the county fair. If you weren't there, it was 'cause you had a darned good reason. The tractor pull would start at 9 o'clock sharp. It wouldn't end 'til there was only one tractor left. The motors on the tractors wouldn't be small. The motors couldn't be quiet. There'd be a lot of dust, noise, and danger. Everyone wouldn't enjoy this event, but my friends and I wouldn't miss the tractor pull for anything.

Dialect, page 51

"I don't <u>rightly</u> know where you <u>git</u> that <u>idee</u>, <u>ma'am</u>," drawled Tex. "We <u>bin</u> <u>tryin'</u> to <u>he'p</u> these <u>ol'</u> boys as <u>bes'</u> we <u>kin</u>."

Maryanne smiled her sweetest Georgia smile and said, "Why, Tex, whatever could give you the idea that <u>li'l</u> <u>ol'</u> me would suspect a big, strong man like you? <u>Y'all</u> know that the <u>guv'ner</u>, bless <u>'im</u>, wants me to investigate why this nasty <u>ol'</u> pipeline contract is so far behind schedule. Without that pipeline, the steel mill <u>kain't</u> open. <u>An'</u> the <u>guv'ner</u> did promise all <u>them</u> people jobs."

"Now, <u>darlin'</u>, don't you worry <u>yer</u> pretty <u>li'l</u> head <u>'bout</u> that pipeline <u>bein'</u> done on time," Tex answered. "We'll have that steel mill up and <u>runnin'</u> <u>'fore</u> that <u>'lection</u>."

Maryanne smiled sweetly, but her eyes sparkled like daggers. "Tex, <u>deah</u>," she warned, "you <u>kain't</u> <u>hardly</u> <u>b'lieve</u> how utterly unpleasant I <u>kin</u> be if <u>y'all</u> are even one day late!"

Possessive Nouns, page 52

Ross's mom was pleased that all the kids at school liked Ross's new jacket. His jacket's lining was red and yellow, the same as their school's colors.

Another cool thing was the new computer game's graphics. Leroy's Digital Dugout was the only place that had the game. At the Dugout, the light's reflection off Ross's new jacket matched some of the game's graphics, as if the jacket's designers copied the computer people's design. But how could cloth match a computer screen's color and graphics? All the kids thought that the jacket's designers must be awesome. Ross's mom's smile broadened as she whispered to herself, "Yes, I'm awesome!"

Possessive Nouns, page 53

1. women's
2. students'
3. parents'
4. butterflies'
5. fans'
6. planets'
7. books'
8. governors'
9. teachers'

Possessive Nouns, page 54

1. a pig's breath
2. the cherries' pits
3. Jason's warts
4. the morning's quiet
5. a month's delay
6. dental floss's strength
7. a year's time
8. a hair's length
9. a day's journey
10. an octopus's tentacle
11. a century's passing
12. an ox's nostril
13. an idea's worth
14. a box's width
15. freedom's price
16. spring's coming

Joint or Individual Ownership, page 55

1. Mark and Sam's locker
2. Mark's and Sam's jackets
3. principal and vice-principal's inspection
4. Maria's and Angela's assignments
5. Maurice's and Emil's backpacks
6. Mark and Sam's door
7. principal's and vice-principal's feet
8. principal's and vice-principal's eyeballs
9. Mark and Sam's offer

Organizations, page 56

1. Barney and Bayleaf's Circus
2. Roscoe Purity's® Cat Chow
3. Dewey, Cheatham, and Howe's law firm
4. Setup and Fail's temporary help agency
5. Hardly-Davidson's newest motorcycle
6. Larson and Moore's repair shop
7. New York City's and Chicago's crime rates

Words with Hyphens, page 57

1. vice-president's sneeze
2. great-grandfather's beard
3. ex-mayor's socks
4. sister-in-law's recipe
5. president-elect's hobby
6. brothers-in-law's jokes
7. stand-in's performance
8. AFL-CIO's rules
9. vice-chancellors' portraits
10. pick-me-up's power
11. jack-in-the-box's handle
12. June twenty-third's party

Indefinite Pronouns, page 58

1. nobody's fault
2. anyone's turn
3. somebody's special guy
4. others' problems
5. Everybody else's time
6. everyone's attention
7. anybody's time
8. somebody else's life

Possessive Pronouns, page 59

We colonists came from a dying planet. Our lush forests had long since been harvested for lumber. Oxygen, therefore, was a scarce resource. On our home planet, huge utilities claimed a monopoly on all oxygen generation. They charged us outrageous fees for the right to breathe their oxygen.

We crossed galaxies and solar systems to find our new home. At last we landed our ship on the planet Vern. A dwarf sun's rays were casting their warmth over the land. As space colonists, we believed our right to control things extended beyond Vern's land. We wanted to guarantee all people's right to breathe air without paying for it. Since there were so few people on Vern, their need for breathable air was far less than their supply. We planned to take their extra air for our own use. The natives didn't seem to understand that we wanted to buy their air. They didn't even know that anyone could own air.

Tricky Pronouns, page 60

1. Who's
2. It's
3. its
4. whose
5. it's
6. it's
7. whose
8. whose
9. who's
10. It's

Certain Plurals, page 61

1. DC-10's
2. PCP's
3. MP's
4. MP's, M-16's
5. GS-13's
6. 10-K's
7. SQ-25's
8. I's, T's
9. 9's

Proofreading, page 62

Mike was a pilot for Ace Corporation. Ace Corporation owned his plane, and it was its job to decide who would fly which routes. Mike thought he always got the worst assignments. He told a friend, "Everyone else's plane airlifts interesting people or grateful millionaires. I'm gettin' tired of always gettin' stuck with the worst cargo to airlift. When it's my flight, it's never a good assignment."

One day, Mike went to talk to the woman in charge of assigning flights. "Let's face it," complained Mike, "Im never in the runnin' for the gravy routes! There's got to be a way to give me some easy assignments!"

That's how Mike was assigned to airlift some pets from Montserrat's disaster area. The Corporation figured he'd have no one to listen to his complaints. They also figured that a three-hour flight in a DC-3 with the engine's roar and the animals' noise would cure Mike's complaining.

Mike picked up a cat, a dog, and a parrot in Montserrat. The flight back was anyone's worst nightmare. With a cat's meowing, a dog's barking, and a parrot's cackling in his ears, Mike was anxious to land the flying zoo safely. Mike's landing was less than perfect, but it would do. It would also be his last for Ace Corporation, he decided.

Commas

Quiz, page 67

1. On January 15, 1963, Rev. Martin Luther King, Jr., gave his most famous speech.
2. Dr. King led a march from Selma to Montgomery, Alabama, in 1965.
3. My oldest sister, Gloria, is more interested in historic events than I am.
4. Yesterday(,) I told her, "Everyone will laugh at you if you wear that dumb skirt."
5. She always says she doesn't care what people think, but I don't believe her.

100% Punctuation

6. Well, if that's what she wants to wear, let her go ahead.
7. If Gloria had any sense, though, she would follow my advice.
8. Gloria, who is fifteen, thinks she knows everything in the world.
9. Gloria may be older than I, but she has more to learn about things.
10. I know, for example, much more about shopping, using makeup, baking, and boys.
11. All Gloria ever thinks about is history, political events(,) and dirty, oily engines.
12. Uncle Jake from Las Vegas, Nevada, taught Gloria all about car engines.
13. He collects cars, old motorcycles, farm tractors, and racing cars.
14. Instead of collecting old junk, I wish Uncle Jake collected cool comics.
15. "Georgie, I hope you've finished your homework," Mom said.
16. I told her I'd get back to it right away, but it won't be easy.
17. How does my mom, the daydream detector, know when I'm daydreaming?

In a Series, page 69

1. You can choose red, blue, green, or yellow M&M's®.
2. Call it candy, chocolate, treats, or dessert, I like them all.
3. I'll eat pies, cakes, cookies, and brownies.
4. *Large, fat, husky,* and *ample* are words others use to describe me.
5. I prefer to think, act, and consider myself *impressive*.
6. I eat, snack, devour, and inhale, therefore I am.
7. They want me on the wrestling, football, and tugging teams.
8. If it isn't eating, sleeping, resting, or snacking, I'm not interested.
9. Coaches would just want me to jog, exercise, work, and practice.
10. As someone famous said, "Give me cupcakes, brownies, and doughnuts, or give me death."

In a Series, page 70

1. All right, I don't like wilted salad, gooey okra, stale corn bread, or grits for lunch.
2. I'd rather have crisp salad, raw carrots, fresh corn bread, and juicy watermelon.
3. If I can evaluate a lunch menu, figure out what's wrong, and propose a better menu, why not do it?
4. Too many people hold back, say nothing, and let problems grow larger.
5. If a menu includes poor choices, unhealthy foods, or stale choices, let's just say it.
6. If no one wants leftover mystery meat, raw meat, or smelly cheese, let's just say it.
7. I value simple honesty, directness, and absolute truth.
8. Yet I also know I should be open-minded, kind to others, and tolerant of others' preferences.
9. My brother says I am overly critical of others, too judgmental, and quick to find fault with just about anything.
10. He says I should spend more time praising others, being grateful for what I have, and looking for the good in everything.
11. I guess being positive about the cafeteria food, complimenting the dietician, and finding at least one thing to like on each menu would be a place to start.

In a Series, page 71

1. In tonight's game, you'll see the agony and ecstasy, the effort, the success, and the drama of human competition.
2. For brunch, we serve rolls, tea, bagels and cream cheese, doughnuts, and coffee.
3. The music selections are country, rock and roll, blues, or jazz.
4. You should pack your underwear, shoes and socks, shirts, pants, and a hat.
5. While returning from Cleveland, we encountered rain, wind, thunder and lightning, hail, and snow.

6. This is a land of milk and honey, opportunity, abundance, and hope.
7. Diana cared for those without homes, the rejected, the sick, and all others, too.
8. For lunch, I'm having a peanut butter and jelly sandwich, juice, and a cookie.
9. Deena's favorite makeup shades are light pink, peaches and cream, auburn, and fawn beige.

In a Series, page 72

1. Wally planned to go to the store, pick up the groceries, and return home by noon.
2. That was before Ralph showed up, took over his car, and changed all the plans.
3. Ralph wanted to drive to the beach, check out who was there, and catch some rays.
4. When they got to the beach, a volleyball game was just getting started, teams were being selected, and they needed two more players.
5. Ralph loved spiking the ball, digging for saves, and blocking other players' spike attempts.
6. Wally enjoyed keeping score, going for drinks, and keeping out of the way of the volleyball.
7. Ralph thought they made a good team, since they stayed out of each other's way, did different things, and he got all the attention.
8. As he drove Ralph to the hospital, Wally agreed that Ralph's final shot would have been great, made volleyball headlines, and gotten Ralph a spot on the Olympic team if Ralph hadn't tripped over his feet.

In a Series, page 73

1. At the hospital, Ralph went on and on and on.
2. He had to tell everyone about his great shot and his great moves and his spectacular ability.
3. Wally was glad to be out, finished, and on his way home.

100% Punctuation

4. Ralph could find someone else to take him home tomorrow and listen to his stories and sympathize with his incredible bad luck.
5. Wally liked Ralph when he wasn't bragging, seeking attention, or hogging the limelight.
6. When Ralph was unsure of himself or uncomfortable with the situation or with completely new people, he was hard to take.
7. He would overcompensate by talking loud or laughing boisterously or trying to be Mr. Charm.
8. If he would just be himself, take it easy, and let other people tell about themselves, more people would like him.
9. Wally didn't know if he should tell Ralph straight out or let him be or give him subtle hints.
10. Ralph was running low on friends and running out of chances and running out of time.

In a Series, page 74

(,) indicates optional punctuation
1. When you go scuba diving, be sure to bring tanks, a wetsuit, a mask, a snorkel, and a regulator.
2. Some of the different types of diving are wreck diving, cave diving, night diving, and ice diving.
3. You can dive in rivers, lakes, quarries, and the ocean.
4. Diving is for men, women, girls, and boys.
5. There are specialty courses for navigation, deep diving, photography, and rescue diving.
6. Some of the skills beginning divers learn are using a snorkel, clearing your mask, and doing the fin pivot.
7. There are ratings for open-water diver, advanced diver, rescue diver, divemaster, and instructor.
8. People dive in the Caribbean, Pacific, Atlantic, and Indian Oceans.

In a Series, page 75
1. Emil's incredible, difficult, long hike
2. a long, hot, humid summer evening
3. Gene's dirty, old, smelly slippers
4. an exciting, free rock concert
5. a sudden, loud, piercing thunderclap
6. tangy, fresh, delicious brussels sprouts
7. a valuable, engraved gold locket
8. an awesome, mysterious, surprising trick
9. the amazing, new, totally fat-free, chocolate dessert
10. Marty's long, boring campaign speech

In a Series, page 76

(,) indicates optional punctuation
1. There are many computer geeks, powerful computers(,) and network connections at the Micro Café.
2. Slide Rule Louie had cool moves, fast fingers(,) and the best brain on the block.
3. The delivery of keyboards, color monitors, modems, and disk drives was received with excitement.
4. With new equipment, would Slide Rule Louie create new programs, games, software solutions, or simulations?
5. When Louie starts cooking on the keyboard, you see flying fingers, wild colors(,) and cool animation.
6. As Louie walked into the Café, people stopped, moved closer, stared, and tried to guess what he would do.
7. Among those around Louie were Brad, CD Charlie, Pat, Mousepad Mike, and Harry.
8. Louie had his books, handwritten notes, floppy disks, and CD's.
9. The anticipation, quiet(,) and expectation hung heavily in the air.
10. Slide Rule Louie was ready to make awesome magic, creative code(,) and fun games.

Nonessential Information, page 77
1. My dog, who is five years old, is not the smartest animal in the world.
2. Last Saturday, my mom's day off, was a case in point.
3. It all started, as you can imagine, at breakfast.
4. Mom, always planning, wanted to know what we were going to do.
5. The we, to be specific, was the dog and yours truly.
6. Rather than keeping quiet, as a smart dog would, Bowser jumped up and wagged his tail.
7. Bowser's tail, which is quite bushy, started dusting the kitchen table.
8. In most cases, especially when Mom's around, that would have been fine.
9. Bowser's tail swept the dishes, not yet cleaned that morning, to the floor.
10. Then Bowser, who has a huge tongue, began licking the food off the broken dishes.
11. That, my friends, is just one reason Bowser hasn't won awards for intelligence.

Introductory Words and Phrases, page 78

At this rate, we'll never get where we're going. You see, every time my dad sees a garage sale sign, he has to stop. Why, you never know when there might be an undiscovered treasure. In fact, we have never yet found any treasures. However, that doesn't stop Dad. No, sir, he checks out every single garage sale. Clearly, there will not be a garage sale left unexamined by his eager eyes. As you may notice, our car keeps getting loaded down with more and more things. Remember, these things are not junk. No, indeed, they are potential treasures awaiting discovery.

100% Punctuation

Interjections, page 79

(,) indicates optional punctuation
1. <u>Watch out</u>! A space alien is landing. (!)
2. <u>Oh, my goodness</u>, it certainly has a lot of heads. (!)
3. <u>Wow</u>, (!) I've never seen such shiny boots. (!)
4. <u>Fifteen feet</u>, that's a whole lot of shoes to buy. (!)
5. <u>Wahoo</u>! It looks like a one-alien, foot-stompin' parade!
6. <u>Wait</u>! If it has two stomachs, will it have two belly buttons?
7. <u>Man</u>, how many eyes are in each head?
8. <u>Hmmm</u>, with four eyes, how would it hook on eyeglasses?
9. <u>Hold on</u>, would you call it "eight eyes" if it had glasses?
10. <u>Watch it</u>! Don't call the alien "eight eyes" if it can hear you.

Prepositional Phrases, page 80

(,) indicates optional punctuation

W. C. Fields (1880?-1946) was a great film comedian. Among the memorable things about his comedy style, many of his sarcastic comments are still well known. On his tombstone(,) his epitaph reads something like "All things considered, I'd rather be here than in Philadelphia." With such an epitaph(,) W. C. Fields didn't seem fond of Philadelphia. I, on the other hand, like Philadelphia quite a bit. For example(,) near the historic district, the mint is a fascinating place to visit. The cobblestone streets of the old town are now bumpy alleys and walkways. On my way home from school on some afternoons, I take shortcuts through these alleys and walkways. Once(,) I tried to ride through them on my bicycle. In no time, as you can imagine, I was bounced out of my skull. Maybe W. C. Fields liked riding on his bicycle. Above all other reasons, that might be why he chose that epitaph.

Adverb Clauses, page 81

Whenever we took my kid sister Harriet out in public, she always embarrassed us. Even if you tried really hard, you couldn't imagine more outrageous outfits than she wore. After a few embarrassing events with her, my brother and I vowed never to go out in public with her again.

Since she knew we were concerned about her outfits, one day Harriet dressed up like a fairy princess. Although that seemed harmless, Harriet was no ordinary fairy princess. Whenever she heard a bell ring, she would wave her fairy wand and bong people on the head. As long as we kept walking very fast, no one got very upset. Until we stopped for the light on Fifth Street, we thought we could get Harriet home without major problems. As if time had stopped, this light would not turn from red to green. As we waited for the light to turn, an ice cream truck came toward us. Before we could cross the street, Harriet heard its bell. Though I'd like to continue this story, my head pounds just thinking about it!

Appositives, page 82

1. Melissa was brought up by the right people, <u>the perfect manners people</u>.
2. They, <u>the perfect manners people</u>, wouldn't even think of using the same fork for both salad and dessert.
3. When they eat or drink, they always hold the pinkie, <u>the smallest finger</u>, higher than the other fingers.
4. They say, "Good breeding, <u>the right stock</u>, always shows."
5. Melissa, <u>our sister</u>, always asks permission before leaving the dinner table.

6. She, <u>Melissa</u>, makes my brothers and me sick.
7. We, <u>the cool guys</u>, think manners that don't make any sense are stupid.
8. Melissa counters, "You, <u>my ignorant brothers</u>, need so much training that it's not worth the effort.'
9. Wait a minute! Melissa, <u>our snooty sister</u>, has the same parents we do.
10. If having perfect manners is genetic, <u>inherited from your parents</u>, we're doomed!

Appositives, page 83

1. Maureen wanted to see the movie *Action on the Bloody Frontier*.
2. John wanted to see a more romantic movie, *The Promise of Love*.
3. Maureen wondered what John, her friend, was thinking.
4. Last week, Maureen had seen the movie *The Monster Who Ate Everyone* with Jason, another friend.
5. Jason, Maureen's preferred movie companion, considered himself her only boyfriend.
6. Of all the boys she knew, though, Maureen's favorite was her friend John.
7. Perhaps she could transplant Jason's bloodthirsty movie taste into her favorite boyfriend, John.
8. John, the chosen boyfriend, had no idea he was Maureen's favorite boyfriend.
9. John asked Maureen out to see the movie *Run, Girl, Run*, but she was busy.
10. After seeing Maureen with Jason, John, a very confused fellow, stopped asking Maureen out.

Direct Address, page 84

1. Karim, we have to get serious about building this great pyramid.
2. We need more water, Rafi, for the workers.
3. The logs, Faisal, must be delivered over here.

100% Punctuation   167   Copyright © 1998 LinguiSystems, Inc.

4. Well, now, Joseph, how many slaves will arrive today?
5. Yasir, locate living quarters for the new arrivals.
6. Has the limestone quarry run out of stone, Abdel?
7. Get enough slaves, Ptolemy, to ensure that there is plenty of stone.
8. I want you, Habu, to get the hemp woven into hauling ropes.
9. Amun of Thebes, you bring me good news about the stone masons.
10. We will use your camels, Sheik Hammad, for hauling stone up inclines too steep for slaves.
11. Ah, Cleopatra, it is no fun organizing the building of a pyramid.

Parenthetical Comments, page 85

1. Mary Jane, in fact, was the most sarcastic person in the world.
2. There was nothing, and I mean nothing, that she wouldn't say.
3. If it came into her head, small head that it was, she would say it.
4. It didn't matter who, including family, she offended.
5. She would smile such a sweet little smile, naturally, before she nailed you.
6. Then she met, if bumping into someone is meeting, Bad-Mouth Bob.
7. Bad-Mouth Bob, as you may have guessed, had the worst mouth around.
8. He wasn't just disgusting, although he was that, he was also mean.
9. He was, to understate it, downright cruel.
10. When they met, it was love, although it seemed more like war, at first slight.
11. Did you catch, by the way, the pun at the end of sentence ten?

Tag Questions, page 86

1. We don't want me to get angry, do we?
2. You wouldn't want me to get wet in this rain, would you?
3. I know you care for me, don't you?
4. It's true no one is happy when I'm miserable, isn't it?
5. Let's see if we can find a solution, shall we?
6. I could ride in your nice, dry car, couldn't I?
7. That wouldn't get your seats too wet, would it?
8. After all, I am your superior, aren't I?
9. This is a fine situation, isn't it?
10. You can't believe they drove off and left me, can you?

Contrasting Elements, page 87

1. The twins like fast-paced action games, <u>not mind games</u>.
2. They liked playing with people who couldn't tell them apart, <u>not people who knew them</u>.
3. These people thought the twins moved too fast for one person, <u>more like two people</u>.
4. Hide-and-seek, <u>unlike dodgeball</u>, was perfect for the twins.
5. Only one twin, <u>never both</u>, could be with the other players at a time.
6. When a twin was a hider, <u>not a seeker</u>, the plan would work.
7. The known twin would run away from, <u>never toward</u>, the hidden twin.
8. The seeker was being watched by two twins, <u>not just one</u>.
9. When the seeker got close to one twin, <u>as opposed to the other</u>, the fun began.
10. That was when the hidden twin could run, <u>never walk</u>, to home base.

Dates, page 88

On March 10, 1990, a statistics professor told me this math trick. If you ask 30 people for their birthdays, the odds are very good that two of them celebrate their birthdays on the same date each year. The first time I tried it March 11, 1990, it worked like a charm. Something reminded me of this trick last week, just in time for our neighborhood block party. That would be a great time to try it again, even with only 28 people.

Once I explained the trick to everyone, we started making a list of our birthdays. I was born on August 26, 1989, in Albany, New York. Geno Rizzo was born on May 10, 1990, in Syracuse. His brother was born April 19, 1992, and his mother was born April 21, 1964. Kareem Jackson was born June 5, 1989, in New York City. His dad was born January 6, 1966, during a blizzard. Yolanda Royce was born on August 26, 1990. It worked! Yolanda and I both share the birthday August 26.

Try it with your class or your neighborhood. Make a list of the month and date of everyone's birthday. I bet at least two people in your class have the same birthday!

Addresses, page 89

1. Is 235 North Main Street, Springfield, Missouri, your current address?
2. You were clocked in front of 126 Maple Street in Wilton, Iowa, going 55 miles per hour.
3. From there to 360 Maple Street at the edge of town, Wilton is a 35-miles-per-hour zone.
4. I trailed you all the way to 777 Unlucky Boulevard here in Tipton, Iowa.
5. You may pay your fine at 100 West Main Street, Des Moines, Iowa.
6. Your court date is September 12, 1999, at 333 1st Street in Des Moines.
7. If you can't afford a lawyer, contact the public defender at 10 2nd Street, Des Moines, Iowa.

100% Punctuation

8. I suggest the safe driving school held at the Mercer Building, 1515 26th Avenue, Moscow, Iowa.
9. The people at the Safety Institute on 300 Chevrolet Drive in Detroit, Michigan, want you to use your seat belts.
10. You may get your license after posting bond at 1223 Headquarters Avenue, Wilton, Iowa.

Letter Openings and Closings, page 90

1. Dear Ms. Workmehard,
   Very truly yours,
2. Dear Dad,
   Your loving son,
3. Dear Mom,
   Sincerely,
4. Dear Dynoblast,
   Yours truly,

Titles, page 91

1. Harry B. Doubtful, M.D., didn't believe he was the father of his children.
2. Robin Graves, Ph.D., wanted DNA samples to prove whose child was whose.
3. Harry's wife, Ann E. Mall, DVM, was angry with her husband.
4. Harry thought Will B. Brief, LL.D., would be the best lawyer for marital problems.
5. Ann thought marriage counseling with Mary N. Haste, Ph.D., would be better.
6. Harry and Ann called their friend Len D. Money, CPA, for his opinion.
7. Len D. Money, CPA, said, financially speaking, Ann and Harry should stay married to each other.
8. Mary N. Haste, Ph.D., knew she could save the marriage.
9. Will B. Brief, LL.D., didn't agree, so he consulted a social worker.
10. Sylvia Lining, MSW, insisted that Harry and Ann learn to talk to each other honestly.

Compound Sentences, page 92

(Answers may vary.)

1. There will be a test tomorrow, so I should study tonight.
2. Mrs. Lincoln is not an easy teacher, and her tests are hard.
3. My favorite TV show is on tonight, and I want to watch it.
4. I'm responsible for myself, so I have to decide whether to watch TV or study.
5. Tonight's show is about dinosaurs, and the test is on geography.
6. I like dinosaurs, but I also like geography.
7. I could just watch the show, or I could study before the TV show.
8. That is a good solution, so there is no problem.

Compound Sentences, page 93

1. We had been gone for days, so our dog, Rascal, was happy to see us.
2. We opened the car door, and Rascal jumped right in.
3. The window wasn't open very far, so Rascal couldn't jump out.
4. He slobbered everywhere, so I'd have to clean up the drool all over the car.
5. His hair was all over the back seat, so someone would have to vacuum it.
6. I offered to clean up the drool, but my brother didn't offer to do anything.
7. Rascal started barking, and Mom told him to calm down.
8. We laughed, but Mom didn't see the humor.

Compound Sentences, page 94

1. I'm not a picky eater, so I'll try anything.
2. You took that smelly cheese out, so I'm leaving.
3. I said I'd eat anything, but I was wrong.
4. I won't eat that smelly cheese, for it smells as bad as it looks.
5. Put that ugly, smelly cheese away, or I'll leave.
6. Now the whole room stinks, so I can't stay.
7. You're going to open a window, for you think the smell will go away quickly.
8. You ate some of the stinky cheese, and your breath still smells awful.

To Prevent Misreading, page 95

1. Once the mixture is blended, add the sifted flour.
2. Aware of the noise, the band leader closed the door.
3. She who laughs last, laughs best.
4. But for a tense second, the audience enjoyed the performance.
5. A ring, on the other hand, would be too expensive.
6. Once discovered, caves with fine caverns can become famous.
7. Now refreshed, the hikers continued their dangerous climb.
8. Earlier, bus passengers could get change when they paid their fares.
9. Once revolutionary, telephones and TV's have become routine home equipment.
10. While we were kicking, the principal visited our swimming training.
11. With children around, sharp things can be dangerous.
12. For once, Brad's shoes are tied and his socks are clean.
13. Not knowing for sure, I guessed at the answer.
14. By the way, she already asked someone to walk her home.
15. Suddenly famous, Rachel had to wear sunglasses and a hat to avoid her fans.
16. With exercise, athletes' muscles get even stronger.

Run-on Sentences, page 96

1. I am always late for the class after gym class, since the room is clear on the other side of the school.
2. If I don't take a shower, I can make it to class, but everyone in the class would wish I didn't make it.

3. My choices are to be late or to be stinky. That is not much of a choice.
4. In the summer, I can go outside and take a shortcut, but that doesn't help me in the winter.
5. I think the principal set up my schedule. I always get in trouble, and it seems I have to visit her every day.
6. She said she doesn't want to see me in her office again for being late, so I asked her how I can get from one end of the school to the other.
7. The principal looked at my schedule. She asked how it got set up this way.
8. She moved my gym class to the end of the day, and that solved the problem.
9. Maybe the principal didn't set up my schedule to get me in trouble, but she was good about fixing it.
10. I guess principals can be helpful, too, but none of my classmates had better hear me say that, or I'll lose friends forever.

Proofreading, page 97

I'll never forget Saturday, June 11, 1994. It all started out normally enough, and I thought it would be a lazy summer Saturday. That was before Larry Minton, Ph.D., showed up at my apartment at 522 West 23rd Street, Minot, South Dakota. You wouldn't think that one person could spoil a day, would you? Well, you just don't know Dr. Minton. Someday, maybe even in this century, I'll be able to meet with Minton without any disasters. If you think we were going to have a normal meeting that Saturday, you're wrong.

It didn't matter to Larry that I had to mow the lawn, clean the garage, pick up the mail, and get groceries. No, that conceited, arrogant, pushy, vain Larry wanted his special problem to take center stage. Although I tried to tell him I was too busy for another one of his adventures, he told me we were off to the Amazon rain forest in Brazil. He had my ticket, and all I had to do was pack a few things for jungle hiking.

"You know," I protested, "I have a life, too!" Larry explained that he had contacted all of my teachers, and they agreed that a trip to the Amazon rain forest would be an educational experience. They would, furthermore, be happy to allow me to accompany such a renowned anthropologist as Dr. Lawrence Minton.

Well, there you have it, one minute I was going to the grocery store, and the next minute I was on my way to Brazil. The funny thing is, that was the most planned, normal, sane thing that happened to us on that adventure.

Quotation Marks

Quiz, page 101

1. Tristan said, "I don't see anything so messy about my room."
2. "This stuff on the floor and your desk," Dad explained, "is what I'm talking about."
3. Then Dad told Tristan to clean his room before he did anything else.
4. Tristan found his guitar and played "This Land Is Your Land" a few times.
5. Then he called Joel and asked, "Want to shoot some baskets later?"
6. "Sure, let's do it!" Joel said. "What time will you be there?"
7. "As soon as I get released from 'cleaning prison'," Tristan said sarcastically.
8. "While I wait for you, maybe I'll write a poem called 'Cleaning Blues'," Joel suggested.

Direct Quotations, page 103

1. "Why are you pounding so hard, boy?" asked Captain Ahab.
2. "Sir, I'm trying to close the hatch," replied young Abe.
3. "Just use your hands to turn the handle!" exclaimed the captain.
4. "But, sir, it's stuck," Abe responded.
5. No way, just watch me, boy!" yelled the captain.
6. "Oof, ugh!" grunted the captain as he tugged the handle.
7. "Just pound that handle, boy!" commanded the captain.

End Marks, page 104

1. "How long does it take to clean your room?" asked Mom.
2. Brenda responded, "Well, I have to read everything before I throw it away."
3. "Why don't you read it when you get it and then throw it away?" Mom suggested.
4. "You know, your brother's room is always so clean," continued her mom.
5. Brenda sighed, "That's not fair."
6. "He's just a kid," Brenda complained.
7. Mom countered, "I don't see what is so different between you and your brother."
8. "Is anybody home?" shouted Grandpa.
9. "We're over here in Brenda's pigpen," answered Mom.
10. "Reminds me of your room when you were Brenda's age, Doris," Grandpa chuckled.

Interrupted Quotations, page 105

1. "Even just a bus ride," Mark lamented, "is an adventure with you."
2. "We have the police, the CIA, and the Royal Mounted Canadian Police looking for us," Mark continued, "not to mention your former boyfriend."
3. "Mark, dear," Leonetta purred, "it really isn't all that bad."
4. "Not all that bad!" roared Mark. "I don't see how it could get much worse."
5. "You may have started an international incident," Mark pointed out, "just because you didn't want to sit next to a man who smelled like sauerkraut."
6. "But he did smell like sauerkraut," Leonetta complained. "He really did."

100% Punctuation

7. "Yes, but did you have to take his container of sauerkraut off the bus," asked Mark, "and walk into the waiting hands of drug police?"
8. "How was I to know," pleaded Leonetta, "that he had hidden illegal drugs in the smelly sauerkraut?"
9. "I couldn't believe," Leonetta pointed out, "that anyone would open that smelly container."
10. "I'm pretty sure," Mark stated, "that the real smuggler agreed with you."

More Than One Sentence, page 106

"Hello, welcome to Quick Food. May I take your order?" asked the cheery counter attendant.

"Yes, I'll have a Value Meal 2," responded Matt.

"Would you like fries with that?" came the cheerful reply.

"Don't fries come with a Value Meal 2? I mean, if I didn't want fries," Matt grumbled, "I'd have ordered just a burger and a soft drink."

"You don't have to be so grumpy!" the attendant said, a bit less cheerfully.

Matt growled, "Well, maybe I like being grumpy. Especially when I know what I'm ordering and I order it. Then when someone asks me a question she should know the answer to, I get even more grumpy. So are you happy now?"

"Sure, but if you'll look at the menu," the cheery counter attendant explained, "you'll see that a Value Meal 2 comes with a choice of cole slaw or French fries. A value meal with cole slaw is a Value Meal 2a, and a value meal with French fries is a Value Meal 2b. So would you like fries with that?" asked the cheerful counter attendant.

Interrupted Quotations, page 107

1. "I wonder where were you on June 22," said Detective Clueless.
2. "I suppose I have to tell the truth," Bogg replied.
3. Detective Clueless responded, "I don't imagine you'd rather be arrested."
4. Bogg replied, "I thought I heard you say 'digested'."
5. "I wonder if this is a joke," said Detective Clueless.
6. "I was wondering if I could please have some fresh flies," said Bogg hopefully.
7. "I think you mean French fries," Detective Clueless corrected.
8. "Slurp! I wonder if anyone else has a question," said Bogg.

Titles of Short Works, page 108

Our band director says, "If it isn't a Sousa, it isn't a march!" I guess we'll be playing "The Stars and Stripes Forever" forever. We flute players would rather play show tunes like "The Sound of Music." Our English teacher says that the movie based on the book *Gone With the Wind* inspired some great music. With our luck, all we'd get to play from that movie is "Dixie."

Maybe our music teacher could arrange "Sergeant Pepper's Lonely Hearts Club Band" by the Beatles for us to play instead of "Stars and Stripes Forever." We flute players have to work as hard as slaves, but we never get any respect.

Here comes the band director with our new piece, "The 1812 Overture." I wonder how hard the flute part is in this one.

Definitions, page 109

1. In Yiddish, *nosh* means "to eat a small snack."
2. A *haploid*, my dear Watson, is "an organism with but half the normal number of chromosomes."
3. A *mesocarp* is "the part of the cherry you eat between the pit and the skin."
4. Grandpa's favorite expression, *verbum sap*, means "enough said."
5. The word *flout* means "to treat with contemptuous disregard."
6. A *hat trick* means "the scoring of three goals by a single hockey player in one game."
7. *Putsch* means "a secretly plotted and suddenly executed attempt to overthrow a government."
8. A secondary verb meaning of *pestle* is "to beat, pound, or pulverize with a pestle."
9. The word *spoonerism*, named after William A. Spooner, means "a transposition of initial sounds of two or more words," such as *dig bait* for *big date*.
10. A *thaumaturgist* is defined as "a performer of miracles."

Slang or Special Words, page 110

On Starship 587, Elaine took a "sashay" along the space station's flight deck. Captain Hip Rune watched her on his monitors to protect "the li'l filly," as he called her. Hip liked to think of himself as a "man's man," stronger and smarter than any woman. He felt it was his duty to protect women, since they were clearly "the weaker sex." Actually, Elaine was about as fragile as a "pet rock," although Hip was clueless about her strength and her expertise.

Elaine, the station's first engineering officer, was the only one who knew the "Series 5 Acceleration Sequence," so Hip needed her. Hip hated needing some "sweet little thing" to run his manly space station. Besides, Hip was kind of "sweet" on Elaine. He'd just have to show her he was "top dog" so she'd have the proper respect for him.

Hip was daydreaming about Elaine when his elbow slipped and

100% Punctuation 171 Copyright © 1998 LinguiSystems, Inc.

activated the "Intruder Alert" alarm. Elaine was halfway through her Cadet Emergency Drill before Hip knew there was a problem. He saw Elaine securing doors in the corridor outside his command post. Well, maybe he'd just have to "mozey on out" to visit with her. Surely she'd be impressed with his "to-die-for" aftershave.

Quotation within a Quotation, page 111

1. Josh's teacher said, "The excuse 'the dog ate my homework' just won't work this time, Josh."
2. "I can't believe you think I would use those 'weasel words'," answered Josh. "I'm much more creative than that!"
3. "Then just why is your report on the article 'Thousands Flee Flood' not here?" Ms. Lane demanded.
4. "You see, the TV program *Nova*, which is totally educational, had a special on last night," Josh explained.
5. Josh continued, "Their special, 'Flood of the Century', related directly to my report."
6. With her hands on her hips, Ms. Lane said, "I don't care what you watched on TV last night. It's 'zero hour' for your report."
7. Josh gave it one more try. He said, "This is a real 'catch-22'. I can't learn about the flood from TV, yet I'm supposed to write a report about it."
8. "You're in luck, Josh," said Ms. Lane with a smile. "You can sit down right now and show me what you learned from both the 'Thousands Flee Flood' article and the 'Flood of the Century' special."

A Quotation As Part of a Sentence, page 112

1. "Ask what you can do for your country" has become part of pop culture.
2. Boy Scouts aren't the only ones with a "be prepared" approach.
3. "I want you" is said by more employers than just Uncle Sam.
4. The expression "show me the money" came from the movie *Jerry Maguire*.
5. The "you break it, you buy it" policy of Deedee's Gift Shop makes me nervous.
6. My sister always says she needs "just a few minutes" in the bathroom, but she hogs it for at least an hour every morning.
7. I hope you have an "m'm, m'm, good day"!
8. I never get tired of that song, so "play it again, Sam."
9. Don't worry! It's only halftime, and "it ain't over till it's over."
10. Mother Teresa helped people she called "the poorest of the poor."

Proofreading, page 113

"Avast, ye maties!" shouted Captain Bly.

"What does *avast* mean, anyway?" inquired Nate. "I mean, pirate guys are always swaggering around saying 'swabbies' and 'walk the plank' and stuff like that. What does it all mean, anyway?"

"That's true," commented Wil. "If any term is not in the dictionary, we should demand an explanation."

"What be ye maties gibberin' about?" asked Bly.
Editor's Note: As used here, *matie* means "a crew member of a ship." *Maties* is the plural of *matie*. The language in this story is adapted from *Mutiny on the Bounty*, copies of which can be purchased at your local bookstore or checked out of your local library. Now back to our story.

"Ye made me forgit my place," complained Bly.

Wil said, "Yes, an editor can be a nuisance. But your place is not as our captain, Bly. You're more suited to be our cabin boy."

"That'll be 40 lashes for sassin'!" ordered Bly.

Nate responded, "Since Wil and I are the only two crew members, 'maties,' as you call us, how do you propose to carry out your order? Besides, since this ship is really a Sixteen Flags Themepark ride, why don't you knock off the British pirate routine?"

Colons

Quiz, page 116

1. I think my first novel will be *Dating: Don't Even Bother*.
2. I'd like to introduce the world champion maker of toe jam: Ray Hunt.
3. Please bring these things on the field trip: a jacket or sweater, a lunch, sunglasses, and a signed permission form.
4. We'll leave at 10:30 sharp.
5. There's just one thing on my mind: vacation.
6. Use a 3:1 ratio to mix the oil and vinegar.
7. The ingredients are as follows: cooked rice, vinegar, oil, and chicken.
8. I have a huge problem: I've lost my wallet.

Introducing Lists, page 118

1. What we have here is a complete mix-up: no grounds to complain, no violation of any law, and no obvious way to recover.
2. We have experienced the following: misunderstanding, confusion, and danger.
3. To get out of danger, our needs are as follows: a plan, someone to execute the plan, and enough money to fund the plan.
4. We used to have everything: the people, the money, the plans, and the energy.
5. Look what I just found: plans, spare parts, and fuel!
6. Let's divide into three teams: home base, transport group, and forward base.
7. Home base will be responsible for three areas: scheduling shipments, receiving shipments, and repairing vehicles.

8. The transport group will control voyage-specific tasks: operating the shuttle craft, recording outgoing inventories, and recording incoming inventories.
9. Forward base will be responsible for outer space maneuvers: dockings, landings, explorations, and takeoffs.

Introducing Lists, page 119

1. We all need these things: reassurance, understanding, and encouragement.
2. Many of you are looking for the following: a home, a career, and a friendship.
3. You should put aside all of these: your fears, questions, and thoughts.
4. Without thinking, follow these things: your heart, emotions, and feelings.
5. I will lead you to all of the following: places you haven't been, things you haven't seen, and wonders you never imagined.
6. My enemies are as follow: rational thought, critical thinking, and independent reasoning.
7. Just follow these things without thinking for yourself: TV, radio, and magazines.
8. That way, the media will control all of these: your present, your future, and your life.

Long Quotations, page 120

1. The United States Constitution, written in 1787, begins, "We the People...."
2. Abraham Lincoln said in his Gettysburg Address: "Fourscore and seven years ago, our forefathers brought forth upon this continent a new nation, conceived in liberty and dedicated to the proposition that all men are created equal."
3. In 1776, the United States Declaration of Independence justified revolution with these words: "We hold these truths to be self-evident, that all men are created equal, that they are endowed by their Creator with certain unalienable Rights, that among these are Life, Liberty and the pursuit of Happiness. That to secure these rights, Governments are instituted among Men, deriving their just powers from the consent of the governed. That whenever any form of Government becomes destructive of these ends, it is the Right of the People to alter or to abolish it and to institute a new Government, laying its foundation on such principles and organizing its powers in such form, as to them shall seem most likely to effect their Safety and Happiness."
4. During the French Revolution on August 26, 1789, the Declaration of the Rights of Man and of the Citizen was adopted. In Article 4, it says, "Liberty consists in being able to do anything that does not harm others...."
5. The United Nations Universal Declaration of Human Rights adopted in 1948 says: "All human beings are born free and equal in dignity and rights. They are endowed with reason and conscience and should act towards one another in a spirit of brotherhood."

Restatements or Explanations, page 121

1. Our teacher said we cannot have any problems today: the principal is visiting our classroom.
2. This is our big chance: the teacher can't yell at us with the principal around.
3. We each have a plan: I'm going to try something special
4. We will all do something: that way the teacher can't pick on just one person.
5. We are all excited: we have never planned something together before.
6. It is our big morning: we're all going into the classroom.
7. The principal is clueless: he'll never know what hit him.
8. Class, please pay attention: the principal wants to say a few words to us.
9. He is giving us the reason for his visit: he thinks teachers don't use enough strict discipline.
10. We'd better change our plans: we don't want to let our teacher show how strict he can be.

Some Appositives, page 122

1. Uncle Jason is a brick: someone you can always count on.
2. That's what we're laughing at: your drawing.
3. That's what I'm worried about: sneezing without a tissue.
4. Dad writes a cartoon strip under a secret pen name: O. Well.
5. That's my biggest problem: sweaty hands.
6. Trudy finally got what she asked for: privacy.
7. On the floor below the desk was the best evidence: candy wrappers.
8. I'm glad about one thing: no homework for two weeks.
9. My goal for this year is simple: graduate.
10. I knew it was a bad day when the most feared substitute walked in: Ms. Furrchin.
11. My neighbor invented the greatest toy ever: a Whizbo.
12. Share one of life's greatest treasures with others: your cheery smile.

Business Letter Openings, page 123

1. Dear Uncle ___,
2. Dear Super Duper Sounds Company:
3. Dear City Council:
4. Dear Sis,
5. Dear ___,
6. Dear Jenkins Library:
7. Dear Gazette Press:
8. Dear Green Grocery Store:

Character Dialogue, page 124

1. Stan:
2. Oliver:
3. Stan:
4. Oliver:
5. Stan:
6. Oliver:
7. Stan:
8. Oliver:
9. Stan:
10. Oliver:
11. Stan:
12. Oliver:
13. Stan:
14. Oliver:
15. Stan:
16. Oliver:
17. Stan:
18. Oliver:
19. Stan:
20. Oliver:

Groups of Numbers, page 125

1. 12:30 P.M.
2. 1:45 A.M.
3. 3:1 vinegar to soda
4. IV:2:43
5. Psalm 100:1
6. 3:23 P.M.
7. A:B::C:D
8. Vol. 12:1011
9. 2:34
10. 1:45 A.M.

Titles and Subtitles, page 126

1. *Projectile Vomiting: Five Easy Lessons*
2. *Ripped Underwear: Frankie the Ferret Shares His Tricks*
3. *Headlock Tips: How to Survive Close Contact with Armpits*
4. *Acne Agony: Why You Shouldn't Pop Pimples*
5. *Open-Mouth Chewing: Why No One Will Eat with You*
6. *Nose Hygiene: Taming Unruly Nose Hairs*
7. *Toe Jam Is Not Your Friend: How to Keep Your Feet Healthy*
8. *Belching Elocution: How to Talk on Burps*
9. *Bug Patrol: How to Check Yourself for Lice*
10. *Asking for Trouble: Why Tapeworms and Leeches Make Poor Pets*
11. *Gross but True: How the Sweatshirt Got Its Name*
12. *Green Sleeves: An Alternative to Tissues*

Proofreading, page 127

My name is Sergeant Thursday. I wear a badge. I wear a uniform, too: I don't want you to get the wrong idea. Anyway, I'd like to tell you about something incredible: the story of a crime in the West Side.

It was 12:05 AM, and I was working the night watch. My partner, Sydney, had just come back from the delicatessen with these goodies: a salami sandwich, a large soft drink, fries, and an apple pie. I asked him, "Sydney, how can you eat that stuff? It's bad for you."

Sidney replied by quoting the Surgeon General: "The recommended daily allowance of carbohydrates includes some grams from each of the food groups. When a diet restricts the intake of calories, the patient's metabolism slows down and becomes more efficient. Therefore less food is needed to produce energy, and weight loss is not obtained."

That's when the call came in: the call that began our mystery. It was about a robbery over in the West Side. When we got there, they had already collected the following clues: an old shoe, a coat hanger, a chewed dog bone, a rawhide strip, and a Maltese falcon. That's when we came up with the title of the book we would write about this caper: *The Maltese Dog's Falcon: The Night the Chew Toys Got Loose.*

Semicolons

Quiz, page 130

1. It's almost time for lunch; I'll save my snack for later.
2. Sofia can really keep a secret; I always open my big mouth.
3. Our Quiz Whiz team includes Jake, who knows everything; Rhonda, a total brain; Bob, who doesn't know the time of day; and yours truly.
4. I was hoping to sit beside Doug today; however, he's absent.
5. We wrote letters to the mayors of Shreveport, Louisiana; Raleigh, North Carolina; and Tulsa, Oklahoma.
6.
7. I ran here as fast as I could; I hope I'm not too late.
8. Weather can affect your mood; for instance, lots of people feel blue on a rainy day.
9. Some people think a rabbit's foot is lucky; rabbits might disagree.
10. Please turn that music down; otherwise, no one can hear my great speech.
11. I thought my puppy was a mutt; in fact, it's a border collie.
12. The game is almost over, so let's leave; besides, it's about to rain.
13. We walked all the way to Chelsea's apartment; meanwhile, Beth took the bus.
14. I can't decide whether my favorite season is fall, when the leaves turn bright colors; winter, when snow covers the ground; spring, when everything is green and new; or summer, when the days are long and warm.

Separating Independent Clauses, page 132

1. The band concert was over; now they couldn't stop giggling.
2. They went to a local restaurant; how could they read the menu when they couldn't stop laughing?
3. The waiter couldn't speak English very well; he began laughing with them anyway.
4. The girls asked some embarrassing questions; the boys blushed.
5. They didn't answer; the girls asked once again.
6. The waiter showed up at the table again; he heard the question.
7. Now the girls blushed; they began laughing nervously.
8. From the next table, we tried to hear what they said; we couldn't hear it.

Separating Independent Clauses, page 133

1. It was football day; therefore, Hank needed his lucky shirt.
2. They never lost a game when he had his shirt; as a result, all of his teammates made sure he wore it.
3. Today he couldn't find the shirt; in other words, they were doomed.
4. Bobbie Brown, his offensive line leader, told him not to forget the shirt; however, the shirt was nowhere to be found.
5. Hank frantically looked for the shirt; meanwhile, the team waited for him.
6. Hank found a shirt that looked almost like his lucky shirt; consequently, he might be able to fool everyone.
7. He couldn't find his lucky shirt; on the other hand, this substitute shirt might work.
8. He had to try it; besides, a shirt won't win or lose a game.
9. After the game, everyone said Hank's play played a major part in their win; in fact, they had never seen him play better.
10. The team was ecstatic with the win; however, the players still wanted Hank to find his lucky shirt.

In a List or Series, page 134

1. Nikki's ideal man would be someone who would not be afraid to show emotions of happiness, love, or fear; who would be considerate enough to remember holidays, birthdays, and special occasions; and who would spend a lot of money, time, and attention on her.
2. Josh wore baggy pants with a drawstring belt, plaid pattern, and wide cuffs; a shirt with puffy sleeves, plastic pearl buttons, and a starched collar; and black shoes with wingtips, leather soles, and platform heels.
3. Nikki's friends couldn't believe that Josh, a boring nerd, was Nikki's friend; that Nikki, a sharp dresser, would be seen with Josh, a fashion misfit; and that together, a totally opposite couple, they could find things in common.
4. All things considered, everyone concluded that Nikki, an intelligent woman would make up her own mind; that Josh, a somewhat responsible person, would show his true colors; and that her friends, if they wanted to remain friends, would have to become friends with Josh.

Proofreading, page 135

1. In the mall, we stopped at the Sugar Cane, which sells fresh candies, nuts, and dried fruits; The Athlete's Foot, which has sweatshirts, banners, and T-shirts for most teams; and McDoogals, where we had burgers, fries, and milk shakes.
2. My favorite characters in the movie were Fang, a vampire; Doofus, the detective's dog; and Harry Furrball, a werewolf.
3. Dripping with sweat, Brian walked toward the stage to give his speech.
4. Although the teachers have no contract, they decided to keep working.
5. We have everything we need for a great picnic: lemonade, sandwiches, homemade brownies, games, and a blanket.
6. Lester doesn't have a clue about manners; for example, he chews with his mouth open and uses his arm to wipe his mouth instead of a napkin.
7. I'm not supposed to eat chocolate; I eat it anyway.
8. Take Jason with you because he wants to go; besides, you promised you would let him come with you.
9. Many people wear clean underwear every day; I'm not one of them.

Hyphens

Quiz, page 138

1. John F. Kennedy was the thirty-fifth President of the U.S.
2. When the cookies are three-fourths baked, sprinkle them with sugar.
3. Mice are the best-selling pets in the pet store.
4. I can't eat highly spiced food, so I'll have a twice-baked potato, please.
5. Most people are anti-pollution, but not enough people are pro-active about it.
6. One half of our class walks to school and one third takes a bus.
7. *My Life As an Ex-Child* is a hilariously funny book by a well-known author.
8. Soldiers honored the veteran with a twenty-one-gun salute at his funeral.
9. Marcia is highly honored to be president-elect for the birdwatchers' club.
10. Uncle Leo is more well known for his off-color jokes than for his athletic ability.
11. They're building a six-story apartment where the run-down stores used to be.
12. The new anti-drug campaign got off to a first-rate start today.
13. Leon finished the race in one hundred forty-first place for all runners, but twenty-second place for his age group.
14. Have you tasted that smoke-cured ham with the honey-mustard sauce?
15. I'd love to have a half-time job with full-time pay, wouldn't you?

Syllable Division, page 140

1. trou-blesome, trouble-some
2. bat-tle
3. imme-diately, immedi-ately
4. con-tinuing, contin-uing, continu-ing
5. ex-citable, excit-able
6. ex-aggeration, exag-geration, exagger-ation, exaggera-tion

7. mos-quito
8. in-credible, incred-ible, incredible
9. anony-mous, anon-ymous
10. sub-category, subcat-egory, subcate-gory
11. man-nerism, manner-ism
12. ex-planation, expla-nation, explana-tion
13. proof-reading, proofread-ing
14. ex-clamation, excla-mation, exclama-tion
15. in-vestigate, inves-tigate, investi-gate
16. non-classified, nonclas-sified, nonclassi-fied

Compound Numbers, page 141

1. forty-nine, twenty-one
2. seventy-five
3. one hundred fifty-nine
4. forty-first
5. one hundred thirty-two
6. twenty-eight
7. forty-five, three hundred twenty-five
8. twenty-seven
9. seventy-two

Proofreading, page 142

1. Dale was Lisa's mother's ex-brother-in-law.
2. Did that make him her ex-uncle?
3. In the pre-divorce world, he was her uncle.
4. Now that it is post-divorce, is he her nothing?
5. Her most important question was this: Do you get presents from an ex-uncle?
6. She would ask her all-knowing stepbrother, Jeremy.
7. Having already had two mothers, her half brother was the most anti-divorce person she knew.
8. Jeremy said that he might actually be her ex-stepbrother, since her mom was not his mom, and his dad was not her dad anymore.
9. Therefore, Jeremy's dad was Lisa's ex-stepdad.
10. Lisa decided that, if her mother ever remarried, she would be her mom's self-appointed marriage preserver.

Compound Adjectives, page 143

1. It was a little-known fact that Otto was the world's greatest runner.
2. In fact, no one but Otto knew this closely guarded secret.
3. Today was the all-important, first race of what would be his wildly successful career.
4. At the end of today, he would have an undefeated, one-race career.
5. Otto was running what used to be the one-mile race that was now a 1,500-meter run.
6. The 1,500-meter run was still a fairly difficult, middle-distance race.
7. Otto had super-long cleats on his track shoes for extra traction.
8. His lightning-fast start would swiftly propel him into the front runners.
9. Otto wore a blood-red jersey and cobalt-blue shorts, since those were his school's colors.
10. As Otto came to the starting line, he could see a half-lap stagger for each lane.
11. The starter's gun went off; it was time for Otto to begin his world-famous career.

Compound Adjectives, page 144

1. Have you ever had 24-hour flu that lasted 36 hours or more?
2. I need 6-, 12-, 18-, and 24-inch rulers for my art project.
3. There was a five-car collision on our street last night.
4. Why does the military give a 21-gun salute sometimes?
5. Uncle George took an 8-hour dose of cough medicine.
6. There were two-, three-, and four-alarm fires in Chicago last week.
7. I caught a 20-second peek at my sister's two-year diary.
8. We have four-, six-, and seven-story buildings in our apartment complex.
9. My three- and four-year-old nieces are coming to visit.
10. This fan has a four-way switch.
11. I need 24- and 36- exposure films, please.
12. Brian broke his record in the 200-meter run and the twenty-yard dash.

Fractions, page 145

1. One half of the test will be math story problems.
2. That is more than one-half trouble: that is huge trouble for students like me.
3. If a glass is one-third full, and it holds twelve ounces, how many ounces are in it?
4. If there are 12 people, and two fifths of them are blond, how many are blond?
5. How can there be four fifths of a blond person?
6. Can a person be four-ninths alive?
7. If a glass is one-half full, can it be one-half empty at the same time?
8. If John takes Sally for a ride in the country, and if his gas tank is one-tenth full, is John an honorable person?
9. The team concentrated seven tenths on the game and three tenths on the crowd.
10. Pretzel is one-half collie and one-half black labrador.
11. One fourth of the students in our class has an older brother.
12. The track meet was two-thirds over before we won an event.

Preventing Misreading, page 146

1. g
2. d
3. f
4. e
5. c
6. a
7. h
8. b

1. anti-intellectual
2. hydro-ski
3. semi-invalid
4. uncalled-for
5. pre-engineered
6. micro-organism
7. age-group
8. anti-inflammatory

Proofreading, page 147

1. The pitcher was two-thirds full before it cracked into twenty-two pieces.
2. Melissa is anti-desserts these days so she can wear her all-time favorite jeans.
3. Let's go for just a half-hour ride before we re-enter the data for our project.
4. Uncle Mike has a ten-year-old motorcycle in absolutely perfect condition.
5. The taste of our cafeteria food is highly overrated.
6. How loud is a twenty-one-gun salute?
7. Call me at one-thirty this afternoon, before I start my new part-time job.
8. I'll take the eighty-two bus to Thirty-Second Avenue.
9. Neil never thought he'd win a weight-lifting competition.
10. Rodrigo, a well-known bullfighter, is an ex-citizen of Spain.
11. Rodrigo is more well known in Mexico now than in Spain.
12. Four- and five-year-old children have class in the all-purpose room.
13. Dad is one-half English, one-quarter Chinese, and one-quarter Jamaican.
14. Save fifty-five percent at our going-out-of-business sale!
15. If our landlord won't be pro-pet, he could at least be pro-cat or pro-dog.

Italics/Underlining

Quiz, page 150

1. The *Queen Elizabeth II* is cruising the Atlantic this month.
2. Did you see the rerun of "Cold Feet" on *Mad About You* this week?
3. I'm not into piercing toes or kneecaps, but *chacun à son gout*, I always say.
4. How do you spell *judgment*, with or without an *e* in the middle?
5. An article in the *Wall Street Journal* explained the rising cost of paper.
6. My favorite novel is *The Giver* by Lois Lowry.
7. Some people think the number *13* is unlucky; I think they're right.
8. The painter Georgia O'Keeffe had a way of making even animal bones beautiful and graceful, as in her *Summer Days* painting.
9. Oil shale has layers of *kerogen*, a waxy material made of decayed matter.
10. I think *however* is the most boring word in our language.
11. Have you read *Catherine, Called Birdy* yet?
12. Aunt Rosie named her new plane *Herby 2*.
13. After watching the movie *Apollo 13*, I'm not sure I'd like to be an astronaut.

Titles, page 152

1. Chapter 3, "Watermelon Seed Spitting," is the most important lesson in the book *How to Be an Annoying Guest*.
2. We can't wait for the final episode, "Mary Goes to Fargo," on *The Restless Ones*.
3. Everyone listens to *Truck Talk* on our public radio station.
4. The *Wall Street Journal* doesn't have *Beatle Bailey* or any other comic strips.
5. You can't be an Italian-American if you don't know "The Marriage of Figaro" from *The Barber of Seville*.
6. The shortest chapter of the shortest book is "Games to Play on Rainy Days" from *The Sahara Nomad's Guide to Watersports*.
7. Even though Vivian Leigh didn't realize it, the song "Dixie" was around long before the movie *Gone with the Wind*.
8. Let's play *Doom* on Jason's new 856 platinum-plus, macro-media computer.
9. They reviewed the 856 platinum-plus, macro-media computer in the latest issue of *Computing Today*.

Titles, page 153

1. What makes the smile in the *Mona Lisa* painting so interesting?
2. How old was Michelangelo when he sculpted *David*?
3. Goya's painting *The Family of Charles IV* is in a Spanish art museum.
4. Renoir captured the emotion and spray of the ocean in *The Wave*.
5. We like Claude Monet's *The Grainstack (Sunset)*, even though it's just a haystack.
6. I wonder who created the *Dying Warrior* from the Temple at Aegina in 490 B.C.
7. *Bird in Space* is a 54" bronze piece completed in 1919 by Constantin Brancusi.
8. Henry Moore made stone look soft in his *Recumbent Figure* from 1938.
9. *The Bride* by Marcel Duchamp (1912) looks more like a factory to me than a bride.
10. I like Paul Klee's *Twittering Machine*, a whimsical piece in watercolor and ink.
11. How many dots are there in *Side Show* by Georges Seurat?

Titles, page 154

Captain San Holo left Club Far Out and piloted the *Freedom Falcon* through space. He was making the first trip to the Earth's moon since the *Apollo 45* had landed on that lifeless asteroid. On the moon, Captain Holo would rendezvous with the *Liberty II* ship. The *Freedom Falcon* and the *Liberty II* were going to be retrofitted at Morton Moon Base. They would get new thrustors, stabilizers, and gyroscopes that would make them the equal of any Empire cruiser, even the awesome, quad-fire *Maureen O'Banion IV*.

As Captain Holo approached the moon base, he was third in line behind the *Lightning Cruiser* and the *Liberty IV*. It would be a longer

100% Punctuation

layover than he had expected; perhaps he would have time to visit Princess Kwani on the *Venus IX* ship.

Foreign Words, page 155

1. <u>tout à fait</u> - altogether, totally
2. piñata - a decorated jar or object filled with candy or toys and hung from the ceiling
3. <u>pour rire</u> - as a joke
4. <u>nicht wahr?</u> - isn't that true?
5. <u>mano a mano</u> - hand to hand
6. karate - a self-defense art
7. <u>tempus fugit</u> - time flies
8. jurisprudence - a legal system
9. <u>joss</u> - a Chinese idol or image
10. che sarà, sarà - what will be, will be
11. <u>lingua franca</u> - a common language

Words, Letters, or Numbers As Such, page 156

1. It was the biggest game of the season. When the coach sent in the play *split right, 65 left, on three*, I thought it was *56 left*.
2. I missed my block, got hit by the linebacker, and only remember the doctor asking, "Don't you even see the big *E* on top of the chart?"
3. I couldn't even remember if my name was spelled with one or two *L*'s.
4. That linebacker really put some pow in the word *power* when he hit me.
5. After that play, I figured I should change my jersey number from *26* to *18* or some other number people wouldn't recognize.
6. I heard my friends outside in the hall say, "Here he is, room 655. Unless he thought the *6* was a *5*, then it would be room 566."
7. I would never live this down. And what about the word *live*, anyway?
8. Spelled backwords, the word is *evil*; that's what my friends would do to me.
9. Just then our coach breezed in and said, "Lloyd, there's only one word for your play that saved the day: *brilliant!*"

Proofreading, page 158

Lois was always name dropping and saying, "Our family came over on the *Mayflower*." She made me feel like saying, "Yes, well, our family came over on the trawler *USS Tawdry*."

On TV tonight, we're supposed to watch "Courageous Beginnings," an episode of *Our American Heritage*. If it has anything to do with Pilgrims, Plymouth Rock, or Cotton Mather, Lois will use the opportunity to tell us again that her family has a reproduction of the painting *Pilgrims' Landing*, which shows her great-great-great-great grandparents.

Nona says her family came over on the ice bridge across the Bering Straight way before even Columbus and his *Niña*, *Pinta*, and *Santa Maria*. Now, that's what I call being first! But Mom says I should take Nona and Lois *cum grano salis*. C'est la vie, we will just have to live with her.

Here's the issue of *TV Guide*. Let me see when *Our American Heritage* starts. Oh, my gosh! It's three hours long! This had better be mighty entertaining!

References

Bengtson, B., Schouveller, G. and Linderman, B. *Grammar.* Grades 5-8, Basic Skills Series. Grand Rapids, MI: Instructional Fair, 1994.

The Chicago Manual of Style. 13th Edition. Chicago: University of Chicago Press, 1982.

Cleveland, C.G. *Clauses & Phrases.* Eugene, OR: Garlic Press, 1993.

Collins, S. H. *Adjectives and Adverbs.* Eugene, OR: Garlic Press, 1990.

Collins, S. H. *Prepositions, Conjunctions and Interjections.* Eugene, OR: Garlic Press, 1992.

Collins, S. H. *Verbs.* Eugene, OR: Garlic Press, 1990.

Hayes, C. G. *English at Hand.* West Berlin, NJ: Townsend Press, 1996.

Kane, C. *Grammar and Composition.* Lewistown, MO: Mark Twain Media, 1996.

Knoblock, K. *Plain English Series: Punctuation.* Torrance, CA: Frank Schaffer Publications, 1995.

Warriner, J. E. *English Composition and Grammar.* Benchmark Edition. Orlando: Harcourt Brace Jovanovich, 1988.

The World Book Complete Word Power Library. Vol. 1. Chicago: World Book—Childcraft International, Inc., 1981.